Chick Flick
Road Kill

A BEHIND THE SCENES ODYSSEY
INTO MOVIE-MADE AMERICA

Alicia Rebensdorf

SEAL PRESS

Chick Flick Road Kill

A Behind the Scenes Odyssey into Movie-Made America

Copyright © 2006 by Alicia Rebensdorf

AVALON
publishing group incorporated

Published by
Seal Press
An Imprint of Avalon Publishing Group, Incorporated
1400 65th Street, Suite 250
Emeryville, CA 94608

Library of Congress Cataloging-in-Publication Data

Rebensdorf, Alicia.
Chick flick road kill : a behind the scenes odyssey into movie-made
America / Alicia Rebensdorf.
p. cm.
Includes bibliographical references
ISBN-13: 978-1-58005-194-1 (alk. paper)
ISBN-10: 1-58005-194-4 (alk. paper)
1. Motion picture locations—United States. 2. Rebensdorf,
Alicia—Travel. 3. United States—Description and travel. I. Title.

PN1995.67.U6R43 2007
791.430973—dc22

2006030697

Cover and interior design by Domini Dragoone
Printed in the United States of America by Worzalla
Distributed by Publishers Group West

To Mom, Dad, and Cherry Street

Contents

Leaving Oakland

P ortraits on book covers and big screens paint the road as an icon of freedom: endless, unhindered, and devastatingly open. It is a well-cut car ad: two lanes, oozing vistas, and no traffic, unless it's a potential sex partner stopped at the same red light. The road is *Easy Rider*. It's Kerouac. A roving backdrop for high-armed Harleys. A world of quarters for public phones, beer in cans, breakfast in the kind of diners that barely exist, and gas stations where you can't pay at the pump. It's *Thelma and Louise* and it's *Rain Man*. Unkempt hair and perpetually good music. The road is where the act of driving solves things. Like America's yellow brick road, it promises heart, courage, brains, new friends, killed demons, and discovering something you had all along. Like the promise of a high school makeover, it makes us wiser, realer, cooler.

The road, like Mr. Right and Cosmic Fate, is one of the great romances in American media. Except I've taken road trips before, and the American road I've seen is less a sexy two-lane blacktop than an eight-lane monster cut through sprawling cities and suburban growth. It's run not by those Cadillac-finned classics, but by luxury vehicles with none of the personality and all the lousy gas mileage. I know the days of hitchhiking are dead, and though the road might still look endless, I suspect that's because you can no longer tell the difference between start and finish: Freeway distances are less a line from point A to B than a loop from one Arby's to another.

Me, I don't identify as a romantic. Born to a scientific dad and a feminist mom, I've always figured that romanticism is no more than a nice way to say "delusion." And since the entertainment industry is one of the biggest perpetrators of such delusion, I've always made a point of distinguishing its version of the real world from mine. Contrary to the standards on the set, I'm generally comfortable with my size 11 frame. I don't think my singleness is a condition that necessarily needs repair, and though I've occasionally wished for the movies' blissful fade-outs and neat endings, I know life is more work than that. Whether I'm mocking the ease with which TV characters find dates and parking spaces or I'm leaving a theater, critiquing the disparity between a heroine's occupation and her apartment size, I'm comforted to think I'm not a sucker.

Recently, however, I had to question the confidence of this self-image. I had to consider that maybe my media savvy does not nullify its influence. That maybe knowing movies are make-believe is rather different from believing it.

It was the summer of 2001. The spectacle of the winter's election had faded, replaced by the more appropriate warm-weather fare of shark scares and a missing-intern sex scam. Networks were releasing an off-season influx of "reality" programming, and too many movies spun themselves in self-referential satire. Newspapers and magazines rode the trend with worried essays on the media-saturated state of today's youth.

That summer, at twenty-six, I was precisely the age the trends spoke so badly for, and though I enjoyed a trashy reality show as much as the next person, I found I was doing okay. I was single. I was waitressing. My life had settled into a fine rhythm. I suffered the occasional daydream of telling a customer to piss off and a fatigue of conversations that kept stumbling into boy-talk clichés, but I also had an adequate social life and enough random flirtations and hobbies to excite me. I loved my schedule, my freedom, and the conversations I'd have with my friends at the bar next door after work. I also heard enough gripes from my more established peers to know that they were not in a place I wanted to be.

Then again, I was single. I was waitressing. Though I knew life was hard and dull, I couldn't help but feel mine lacked oomph. As my friends' relationships became more time consuming, I found my freedom feeling more like loneliness. Months passed more quickly than I was comfortable with, and the confidence with which I carried myself didn't always permeate as deeply as I thought it should.

Being practical and unromantic, I understood that what I felt was probably nothing more significant or dramatic than a midtwenties slump. But still, being practical and unromantic, I wanted to solve it. If I didn't pine for the relationship or the career—which I honestly didn't think I did—what did I want? Why did I often feel let down? Living in the San Francisco Bay Area, I couldn't say I was pressured by any singular model of success. Neither could I blame my family (although it would have been convenient); they were hardly perfect. Certainly, none of my friends had their shit together. It seemed a cop-out to blame television—I, after all, was smarter than that—and yet when I stepped back, I couldn't deny many of my expectations held a remarkable resemblance to images I saw on-screen.

When people told me of places—say, they'd recently gone to the hospital or the Bahamas—I pictured Noah Wyle in scrubs or Tom Cruise spinning cocktails in the background. Other images had a deeper effect; while I usually scoffed at those credit-rolling kisses, in my weaker moments many of them made me weepy. During a night off watching TV, I couldn't help thinking my life was short of weekly dramas. Its plot development was shoddy and its action and sex scenes far too sporadic.

Still, I resisted. I didn't actually think of myself as so susceptible. Yet if there were any doubt about the strength of my romantic notions, if I needed any further proof I was as gullible as all that, it was no more evident than in the way I hoped to solve it.

I wanted to get away. I wanted to take a road trip.

Now, I knew the popular image of the road trip was a farce. It was too Hollywood, too macho, too hippie, too escapist, and too nostalgic; a picture pursued by young, toned boys expecting it to provide them with answers, or at least reckless sex; an ancient photo America preened itself by, convinced it was a mirror rather than a long-past version of itself; and a portrait whose few female road models were inherently false: buffed out in black, wearing mean shoes, and carting phallic weapons as in some kind of Game Boy porn. Me? I'd never chucked an empty Bud in the back seat. Never got or gave head at the wheel. Never forgot I was a woman and the necessary precautions this entailed: the defensiveness of being alone, the dangers of night, the fallibility of my physical strength.

And yet here I was, stalking car ads and leering at road maps. As if in syndication, scrolling yellow road dividers ran through my head. I harbored images of me—weathered, windblown, and dressed in leather—staring down a two-lane blacktop in some rusty gaping space.

That settled it. I was tired of my every image being the refuse from some since-forgotten flick. I figured I had a choice: I could go to therapy, or I could think of another way to confront my inner romanticism.

Therapy really wasn't my style, but what, I wondered, if I went to the places where my Hollywood images were made, to confront and debunk the images they had fostered in me? I thought of place-specific films that had influenced me growing up, such as *Stand by Me, Close Encounters of the Third Kind,* and *Purple Rain.* Shows and movies that stuck in my head, that might have colored my idea of certain regions and cultures in America: *Northern Exposure. Deliverance,* and *Cheers. A River Runs Through It. Fargo.* I knew, of course, the places would not be like the movies filmed there, but I wanted to learn exactly how. I knew I wouldn't find the "real" America, but maybe I'd find a more three-dimensional one. Maybe by correcting my physical impressions of these places, I'd be able to right the other movie myths in my head, help myself see outside the cinematic frames I'd grown so used to.

So I bought a road map and researched famous filming locations until I had a matrix of points that circled the United States. I gave notice at my job, sublet my room, and told my friends about my trip until I had myself convinced. *Damn,* I thought, it was a clever plan. It gave me a sense of direction. A physical path to follow. And it gave me a sense of purpose to justify a road trip, an activity that otherwise would have been too romantic and too frightening for me to indulge in.

I left that summer of 2001 with a guide to U.S. hostels, money I'd saved in four years of waiting tables, and a heap of warnings. I left with a thousand images of what awaited me and no real idea of what did.

CHAPTER ONE

Stand by Me

TEDDY:
Boy, you don't know nothing. Mighty Mouse is
a cartoon. Superman's a real guy. There's no
way a cartoon could beat up a real guy.

VERN:
I guess you're right. It would be a good fight though.

[STAND BY ME]

I leave my hometown of Oakland, California, on an uncharacteristically clear day. Driving north, I run over roads I know like old albums, appreciating that I know what comes next. Petaluma's khaki grassland. The vines of Sonoma, lined up like chorus girls. The road is also as I know it. Cars merge on narrowing lanes with the grace of mating cattle. Semis and neon cones upstage the placid rolling hills. And while I enjoy the hot inland air that whips through my car's open soft-top, so far it smells less like abandon than cow manure.

I'm driving my Suzuki Sidekick, the Tonka Toy of the automobile industry. It's the kind you often see hitched to the back of RVs like a caboose, incapable of even driving itself. It looks as if it belongs to a Smurfette. But if the Sidekick lacks the sex appeal one usually sees in a road movie, it's sensible. Gets decent gas mileage, has easily accessible parts and four-wheel drive, and there's a board in the back so that I have a secure trunk for my luggage. That and it's black and free of the side splashes that decorate so many Sidekicks. For all my good sense, I don't think I could stomach so much pastel.

As I continue north, the vineyards give way to baked hills and unfamiliar convenience stops. I enjoy the mild revelations of connecting names with place: Ukiah, Willits, the vague memories they bring of childhood camping trips.

I'm less fond of the weird, dull cramp growing in my gut.

There is, of course, nothing to be nervous about. The hot wind feels perfect. That musk in the air is almost sweet. And really, I couldn't be more prepared for this trip. Besides the seventy-eight "Be carefuls" and a suggestion from my mother that I bind my breasts, my going-away gifts included a cell phone, an emergency whistle, eight flares, a first aid kit, a knife, and a can of Mace. Rather than leaving with the proper recklessness—snapping open a garbage bag and tossing in the contents of my underwear drawer—I packed my car with practicalities. I brought things for a four-month trip that I hadn't used in the last four years: mini sewing kits, moist towelettes, Neosporin, and an economy-size box of tampons (as if they were a novelty item exclusive to California). I expanded my car insurance. I got AAA. To my right, several monochromatic cows stand under a tree. *People,* I tell myself, *even single females, do far more dangerous and exciting things than this.* The cows look at me, unimpressed.

The day goes on. As I cross over to the coast and into the woods, the trees grow thicker and taller, and by late afternoon, I find myself in the great redwood forests. These woods used to cover more than two million acres. Now, owing to logging and climate changes, they exist only on this narrow strip of the Pacific coast. I glance up at their necks extending past the fog, a maze of pillars seemingly taller than the sky itself. Then I stare back at the asphalt's double yellow line, willing myself not to throw up. My head spins, my eyes tear, and though I want to eschew comparisons, already I can't help it. Those other road heroes sprung eagerly to their adventures and their stomachs followed right along. Why does mine feel as if it's dragging from my rear bumper, flopping its way up the coastal highway?

I pull over into the town of Klamath. The four-store town is wrapping up its annual salmon festival, and several members of the local

Eurok tribe gather, beating drums. I buy a pack of Tums and a beer and check in at the cheapest-looking motel I can find. Outside, the drumming eases into a patter. Inside, cable is showing a horrid 1980s girl-gets-makeover-and-gets-guy movie. It's utter shit, really. The story line is predictable, the characters are implausible, and the male protagonist's feathered hair looks like a toothbrush gone bad. But I watch it until the credits roll and I'm wiping my eyes. Yeah, I'm a wimp—and, yeah, one with an embarrassing weakness for hackneyed romances at that—but it can't last. I know the script. I will be wiser, cooler, and realer yet.

■■■■■■■■■■

Back when I was congratulating myself for my road trip's many strokes of brilliance, I counted among them the fact that it required little actual research. I set out in part to discover what misconceptions I held about America, so it was important I remained as ignorant as possible. Before leaving, I had skimmed two books on pop cultural landmarks and spent several hours on an online movie database, looking up movie locations and marking them on my road atlas.

In the morning, tired of faking sleep in my Klamath motel room, I pull open my map. The first dot lies a couple hours north of Klamath in the small Oregon town of Brownsville. Brownsville has earned a place on my trip by being the filming location for one of my favorite childhood movies, *Stand by Me*. A story by Stephen King of four preteen boys going in search of a dead body, its version of 1950s adolescence was a backdrop for much of my fifth grade year. The boys gathered over their campfire, debating comic book match-ups and the Mickey Mouse Club's Annette's growing tits. In 1980s Oakland, we relived their leeches scene, swooned over River Phoenix, and practiced popping our cheeks to "Lollipop." Never mind we were also Pushing It to Salt 'n Pepa; that while they were telling "your mama" jokes, we were well into rumored finger-bangs. Or that those boys were a loyal gang of four when mine was a bunch of fickle, frequently bitchy eleven-year-old girls. We had our own late-night confessionals in which we discussed our parents' flaws, our crushes, and hurt feelings. "I won't cry. No, I won't shed a tear," went the title song I recorded off the radio, "just as long as you stand . . . stand by me." What if one of your friends would later tattle your secrets to win over someone more popular? It was still totally true.

Okay, so I've never agreed with the movie narrator that people never have friends like they did when they're twelve. Girls that age bite. But following the coast up toward Brownsville today, remembering how we'd watch *Stand by Me*, I do think it's possible that movies will never be the same. Vern's comb, Wil Wheaton telling Kiefer to suck his fat one—we watched it so much, its jokes and victories felt like our own.

Midway up the Oregon coastline, I turn inland on a small road. It trails a brook through glens of red barns and white churches. The road eventually funnels me into Willamette Valley, another storybook stretch of farms and pastureland. A short stint up I-5 and I turn off again, toward the eastern foothills. Not five miles along, I come to it—a small green bridge with a small town just beyond. I doubt I'd recognize it if I'd just happened by, but now the scene is clear. It's one of the last ones in the movie, after Vern and Teddy have left and Gordie has told us of their inevitable growing apart. Chris Chambers and Gordie have a moment, and the camera fixes on River as he walks away. Fuck, he was hot. Gordie tells of how twenty years later Chambers would try to break up a fight in Burger King, get stabbed, and die on the spot. I wish I could save him still.

■■■■■■■■■

Stephen King originally wrote *Stand by Me* based on his own childhood home in Maine, but although Brownsville was chosen for its likeness to the small fifties town, its roots go back a bit further. Brownsville was originally founded as a depot on the Oregon Trail. As America expanded, so did Brownsville, and by the early 1900s it had risen into a trade center with more than a thousand residents. Having parked my car and read the town's bio on a museum brochure, I see the evidence that remains. A stately Victorian stands on the south side and what looks like an Old Western saloon parks itself at the end of the other. Old-fashioned storefronts and dainty flower baskets line the sidewalks. Were I big on quaintness, I would clutch my hands and squeal some high-pitched sound of delight. Instead, I feel as if I'm walking in a well-groomed ghost town. Rain drizzles. The town's shops are quiet and those sweet little sidewalks are bare.

"Brownsville hasn't changed a bit," says the lady at the counter. After strolling Brownsville's main street for a while, failing to find a pulse, I've come to the museum advertised on the brochure. Compared to the rest of the town, it's a hub. Two ladies sit at a round desk with a pile of binders, recategorizing records of all Brownsville's past residents, while two others run the counter of the three-shelf gift shop. They all sport nearly identical hairstyles and large square glasses that both obscure any distinguishing facial features and give them an uncanny likeness to *Sesame Street* characters.

"It's really stayed true to its historical roots," adds another.

I look around the museum and think it's no wonder. The history of Brownsville is laboriously, if somewhat disturbingly, well documented. Walls display children's old, browned report cards and photos of young miners blackened like the dead they soon became. There are rusted appliances and old framed newspapers, railroad tickets, yellowed census papers, and stiff lace dresses. A small, dark boxcar theater in the back airs Brownsville's two locally made movies, *Stand by Me* and a mid-seventies fright flick called *The Flood,* and around it a series of dioramas replicates scenes from Brownsville's 1900s height. An empty pub. An old kitchen. Inanimate objects pose on the shelves as if in a deserted dollhouse. I find the early-twentieth-century gynecological office particularly haunting. The stirrups seem medieval. The metal tools look like tools of torture. I uncross my legs only long enough to return to the ladies.

"Brownsville has a small-town lifestyle and we want to keep it that way. We don't want the chain stores that are showing up in other places," says one of the women as she hands me a book of laudatory newspaper clips about Brownsville: "A good place to raise kids and a place to raise good kids."

"It's just such a great town," another pipes in. "What brings a young lady like you here, anyway?"

"Oh, I'm just passing through." I'm not sure why I lie—whether I'm ashamed of my mission or because it seems insulting. Worse, when I see a handout on *Stand by Me*'s filming locations, I go so far as to feign surprise.

"I had no idea it was filmed here." Even as I say it, I feel like an ass. "Do many people come here just because of *Stand by Me?*"

"We get Japanese tourists from it. They come and take a lot of pictures," says one of the ladies. The subject makes me shy and I turn back to the scrapbooks.

"Yes, they're quite taken," adds another. The women launch back into Brownsville's loyalty to the past and its thriving future. Everyone gets along just swell. I like the women, really—they're as kind and well intentioned as the puppets they resemble—but they talk like brochures and I don't buy it. I take one of the handouts on Brownsville's filming locations and head out to see it myself.

Rain dampens my hair and darkens the asphalt. I walk down to Pioneer Park, where *Stand by Me's* pie-eating contest took place. In Gordie's story, this is where a kid nicknamed Lard Ass took revenge on his town by inducing a massive vomit-a-thon. Blueberry pie's never been the same to me since. The park is huge; with swings, seesaws, horseshoe plots, an outdoor arena, an indoor rec center, and so much wide open space, it seems all of downtown could fit in it and have room to spare. It's also dead quiet. The only movement is of a water fountain stuck on. It spouts an endless stream of water like an offering to a phantom child. I sit for a while on a nearby bench, but it's not long before that fountain is unsettling and all that space suffocating.

I loop through Brownsville's neighborhoods, where the homes are modest and their front lawns are tended to. On the main street again, I notice half the stores advertise antiques, even the coffee shop, and the freshly painted, cherry-red fire hydrants that grace every block. I don't think I've ever seen so many hydrants nor a town so dedicated to its own preservation. I search the filming map, hoping it will give me a sense of direction. I walk by a house where Gordie lived. I see the oak where their treehouse was built. I note again the view of the town where the boys said goodbye. And sure, it looks like those places. But it isn't. There are no kids talking. No high jinks making. Certainly no fifties music playing and no bullies taking bats to mailboxes. I didn't expect these things, of course, but then how come it feels like a disappointment?

■■■■■■■■■

Nostalgia's always struck me as awfully advantageous, warping a time that can no longer defend or correct itself. It also romanticizes the unattainable, which is precisely the kind of masochism I've come on this trip to combat.

I realize this may sound odd coming from someone has just driven five hundred miles to see the site of one of her favorite childhood movies. If I weren't the least bit nostalgic, I surely wouldn't be here, tracking make-believe boys in a faked fifty-year-old set. Still, when I think about it, maybe that's why *Stand by Me* resonated so. At the time it came out, every other movie seemed to hark back to the fifties. There were the musical tributes *La Bamba, Grease*, and *Great Balls of Fire. Back to the Future* had an eighties kid journeying to his parents' teenage years, and Kathleen Turner went back to her own in *Peggy Sue Got Married.* Middle-aged narrators voiced over *A Christmas Story* and made *The Wonder Years* a hit. But while the adult Gordie could be as wistful as any of those other characters, true to its author, *Stand by Me* also included a dark element they lacked. The boys' families were not as functional as the ones they watched on their black and white sets. Bullies did more than just tease; they wreaked real damage. And even if their towns and friendships were quaint compared to Oakland, I still think *Stand by Me* resonated because it was honest to the emotions of dissatisfaction and self-loathing in preadolescence, exploring the idea of innocence rather than merely paying tribute to it.

I consider this as I check out one of Brownsville's antique stores. It's large and packed into a dizzying collage of artifacts: old action figures, a 1949 book on dating etiquette, several washing boards, and a display of modern candy—cell phone–shaped gum dispensers and lollipops on battery-operated spinning sticks. Fifties items are particularly abundant: rows of old Coca-Cola advertisements, Mickey Mouse Club memorabilia, and pastel Fiesta Ware. No one else is in the store right now—the owner's absence doing nothing to help rid the spooks I've felt throughout this town—and I entertain myself by looking at the fifties guide to dating etiquette. I'm midway through the part about the importance of not putting out, reminding myself why I'm glad I didn't grow up then, when the owner bounces in and chirps hello.

"You want to know the main difference between Brownsville and that movie? We've got some tough guys. I mean real rednecks. We'd kick those little hoods' asses."

You wouldn't think this comes from the man who says it. Kelly's voice is high pitched, he cinches his belt way too high, and his cheeks are off a Kewpie doll. Comfortable with him immediately, I've confided my reason for being here.

"But yeah, it's not that different either. I grew up here in the fifties and the town hasn't changed much."

"You've lived here all your life?"

"Oh, *hell* no," Kelly smiles and leans coquettishly on the counter. I'd swear he's flirting with me if I thought he likes girls—something I say not so much because he seems gay as because he carries himself like a preadolescent schoolboy. Surrounded by his vintage Hot Wheels and G.I. Joes, he fidgets as if he's a ten-year-old at Show and Tell. "I spent my teens here, but then I ran away for thirty years."

Kelly tells me about his years traveling Europe and Asia and his decade on Alaskan fishing boats. Something about his wandering makes me feel better. "But I always knew that when it came to settling down, I'd do it here." He leans in to share a secret: "I just wasn't sure that time would ever come." He winks. What a ham.

"And Brownsville didn't change in all that time?"

"Well, sure. The mills have all closed and those farms that have been in families for over a hundred years can't make it anymore." He still wriggles. "But it's still got that old small-town feel, you know? Plus, our history gives us options. I've had this store for five years now, and I just sold the lot next door to an antiques dealer from San Diego."

And the others? I don't say it aloud, but I wonder how those "real rednecks" feel about kitschy Coca-Cola paraphernalia as a portent of their future.

"People say things shouldn't change, but that's the way life goes." He rests his elbows on his Hot Wheels display. "They need to let go."

It strikes me as a little odd to accuse others of nostalgia when back-dropped by vintage Pez dispensers, but no matter. I enjoy Kelly. On another night, he'd whip up gin fizzes and I'd bring cheese and we'd watch the Game Show Network. It'd be killer. But when he leaves to tend to a phone call and I'm left to wander around his store, almost instanta-neously I feel the same jitters I did earlier. The store is so still. The mini cars lie untouchable in the display case. They feel like a monument to the past, but one that's lost its will to play.

I wave goodbye to Kelly on the phone and follow the road that borders the river, intending to return to my car. On the south side near the bridge, I spot a trail through a thicket of blackberry bushes. It feels familiar and I follow it in. The berries are fat and sweet and I indulge until my picking fingers are stained dark. It stirs my own memory of childhood adventures out of the city, of the innocence in picking some-thing edible in the wild and eating it unwashed.

Besides the trees collecting drizzle and dropping rain, all is quiet. I push my way through several bushes and come to a small bank crowded with undergrowth. Though the scene in *Stand by Me* where they found the body was actually filmed about one hundred miles to the south, this looks just like it. How silent it was when they at last found him, his dead body all twisted and gross. The brook in front of me is quiet and the foliage is thick without seeming feral. The air feels damp and soft and slightly eerie.

For the first time all day, I feel something close to the spirit that marked that film. Standing alone on the bank, I feel free from the tight rein Brownsville holds on itself. And I realize perhaps the town is more like the movie than I gave it credit for: It's precisely the kind of place a kid would want to run away from. That, after all, is the truth that made *Stand by Me* so cool. Innocence is usually not so much lost as abandoned. It avoided the romantic trappings that seem to have Brownsville by the ankles.

I reach for a couple more berries, and they are so ripe they fall apart in my hand. I spot some higher up and, in reaching, inadvertently kick a branch by my feet. Under it is something shiny that causes a chill to slink up my spine. Hesitantly, I pull back the branch. Tucked in the brush is a pair of beer cans—the evidence, I imagine, left by a pair of boys drinking down by the river.

ASTORIA, OREGON

I should've probably left when I walked in the hostel doors and started to spontaneously itch. I could've picked up on the graffiti on the walls or the unusual flooring: a collage of carpet samples and car floormats nailed to the ground. If nothing else, the smell should've certainly scared me off. It smelled like wet dog, bacon, and concentrated urine: moldy, meaty, and strangely acidic.

It has to be my hotel fatigue that keeps me here. Traveling up the coast, I've spent the last three nights in Oregon in those blank rooms, embarrassed by my company: *Dismissed, Change of Heart, Blind Date, Elimidate.* I'd never understood why so many would compete to be the people those shows pick. Unfortunately, any superiority complex gained from watching girls try to outfreak each other on a frat boy's pool table quickly erodes when you realize you've just spent four perfectly good late-night hours watching them. Magnify that by the fact that I came on this trip in some effort to fight TV's influence.

Waking each morning after another marathon, I've felt my hypocrisy like a hangover.

So I was looking forward to a hostel's TV-lessness, its camaraderie. I'm realizing, though, however belatedly, that the one I've come to is more of a residential hotel. And a spectacularly nasty one at that. The manager shows me to my room. The only parts of her T-shirt not blotched with stains are those creased into her body fat. She leads me over the car mats, past rooms' open doors—one's stacked full of birdcages, another emits a strong smell of rot—past a guy wearing only jeans and snakeskin cowboy boots. He has a shaved head and a wife-beater sunburn line. He looks me up and down and hisses, "Peachy."

"You can't lock that door from the inside," the manager says, pointing to the room adjoining the common bathroom, "but Fred usually knocks." When she opens the door to my room, part of her shirt comes untucked from her flesh. Sweat has steeped it a peculiar ocher color. The musk is potent.

She leaves me to the room. I scout a safe spot to put my bag and lie on the bed. I lie still, trying not to move, not to look at the ceiling or the sink growing things in the corner. People yell in the hallway. It sounds like a swearing

competition. I try reading but can't concentrate. I try sleeping but it doesn't take hold. And I think, *I wish to all hell I
had a TV.* For as dirty as those dating shows made me feel,
it's nothing compared to the sheets I'm lying on. I lie still
and focus on the voices yelling in the hallway, hoping my
neighbor's romantic dramas might have those shows' same
palliative effect.

"You motherfucking, cocksucking bitch!" It sounds
like my "peachy" friend. "I've got me a bitch of a woman!
A motherfucking bitch of a woman!"

"Fuckin' fucker. He fucks. She fucks. For shit. Shittin'
shitted to fuck." This one's room is on the other side of the
hotel's U and my blinds are broken open, so I also see him
act it out. "Shittin' Fucker Fuckin' for Shit." He twitches,
gestures, and thrashes his arms around as if in a drug high
or fit of Tourette's.

The rhythmic curses have just lulled me to sleep when
someone else wakes me up. It's about 2:00 AM, and his
shouts down the hallway barely register until he starts fid-
dling with my lock. It rattles metallic and loud. Adrenaline
jolts me, freezes me, beats in my head. The latch clicks over.
I'm very, very awake. He turns the knob and hallway light
floods in, illuminating the gritty details of my room.

"Uh, excuse me, I'm, um, in here."

"Oh, fuckin' shit. I'm really fuckin' sorry."

When I get to my car in the morning, I find that a hotel resident tossing lit cigarettes out an upstairs window has burned a hole in my car's canvas top. Fucker. I patch the hole with duct tape. Then again, my car also has its first battle scar. And it feels hard earned.

CHAPTER TWO

Twin Peaks AND Northern Exposure

"Lots of things are rare in Cicely. Boxed lunches.
Public transportation. Victimless crimes.
It doesn't mean they don't exist."

[JOEL FLEISHMAN, NORTHERN EXPOSURE]

By the time I get to Washington, I've spent almost a week on the road. I've fine-tuned my ability to scout out where, in any given town, a thrift shop would lie. The morning disorientation of motel rooms no longer jars me awake. Outside Seattle, I rest for a couple of days at an aunt's house. I enjoy the easy company, the conversations that don't start from scratch, the free laundry. She likes that I share an appreciation of Julia Stiles movies. We watch *Save the Last Dance,* drinking wine while I fold my clothes.

Interesting, that I've never worn much black, but until I'm sorting my clothes, I hadn't realized how much I packed. That's a lie. I spent weeks laboring over what exactly to bring. Maybe it's more that, a week in, I'm better at admitting why. I can concede now that bringing all that black wasn't just to cut down on laundry. No more than those mean black sunglasses were to prevent eye damage or my beat-up cowboy boots were to prepare myself for an impromptu rodeo.

I can now also make similar admissions about the task at hand. On my way up through Washington, I took note of how the freeway numbers are printed on a silhouette of our first president's head. I counted the forests labeled with logging company logos: SECOND GROWTH DOUGLAS FIR, PLANTED 1995. Like a vintage. Or an apology. It's natural to notice things a place does differently, but I know I didn't do it just out of habit. I did it because I was looking for something different.

Washington's always struck me as a moody and eccentric state— the kind of place that attracted curious people and that was weirdly dark even when the sky wasn't. I never considered the source of this image until I planned this trip and thought of the shows based in Northwestern towns: *Northern Exposure* (though set in Cicely, Alaska) and *Twin Peaks.* Ostensibly based on a Jewish doctor's medical assignment and a young woman's mysterious death, the shows' main story lines really revolved around the eccentricities of their small-town residents. In Cicely, a DJ flung pianos. In Twin Peaks, one lady cradled a log; another had a thing for her drapes, and a dwarf talked backward.

Maybe my love of these shows was a reaction to the eighties, to the too–perfect Cosbys and folks in *Family Ties*. Maybe it was because they coincided with my brother's emerging mental illness, with my trying to find my place in a family and a new high school where I suddenly felt so different. Or I was just flattered by them. They presumed their audience was intelligent, which was the look I was going for at the time.

Whatever reason, they resonated. I knew they were just television, but it was still nice thinking towns like those could exist, places where no one was deprived of a personality, where imaginations weren't hampered and people wore their idiosyncrasies with honor. In the morning I pack my black, leave my aunt's, and head east to where they were filmed. I still know they were just television—a comedy, a twisted fragment of David Lynch's mind. And I'm still not expecting to meet the kind of characters that inhabited those Northwestern towns but—I'll say it now—I'm sort of hoping to.

■■■■■■■■■■

Twin Peaks was portrayed as an isolated outpost of America, but the towns in which the show was filmed—Snoqualmie and North Bend—

are actually less than an hour from Seattle proper. Even crowded with Labor Day traffic, the road to Snoqualmie is so wide and smooth it feels more like a suburban thoroughfare than a mountain pass. At its end is an equally mallish parking lot: turn signals and horns fighting over who got there first. Small Car Syndrome makes me hesitant to enter the fray. I spot several SUVs failing to fit into a sidewalk spot, sneak around, and, in two dexterous turns of the wheel, slide in. When I cut the engine, my car purrs a gloat.

Back home, when I was looking up memorable series and movies, some gave me trouble; sites were limited to a town name or a vague address. *Twin Peaks*'s posed no such problems. The cult that evolved around Lynch's series created elaborate websites detailing everything from precise filming locations to the symbolism of a ceiling fan to photo tributes of the latest annual Twin Peaks Festival. I found the sites disturbing in an impressive sort of way. Their elegies to the show's mix of soap opera, mystery, comedy, sci-fi, and noir, to its movie cinematography and krazy-straw story lines, reminded me just how radical the show was at the time. On the other hand, the fans' follow-through did seem the teensiest bit obsessive. Eleven years after the show's airing, many sites were still being updated and the festivals looked well attended. Pictures showed low-rung *Peaks* celebrities judging the costume contest. The competition looked fierce.

No matter, their directions are damn good. I find the Salish Hotel used as the Great Northern's exterior easily. It's a swanky place without being too annoying about it—its low lines and dark wood do well with the forests around it. It doesn't look very familiar, but I owe that to the crowds and the unfortunate fact that it's manned by doormen. They stand in their clownish bow ties and creepy Gap-greeter smiles, and though I know I'm no better dressed than all the other tourists in flip-flops and car sweat, I feel like a guilty sham. I spy an adjacent path leading to the Snoqualmie waterfalls and head toward it.

The paved track is just as thick with tourists; the falls are mere static under their complaints. A husband argues fuel efficiency with his wife. A six-year-old campaigns for the Starbursts his father garnished for later. I follow the slow shuffle to the falls' vistas. A kid in a Broncos jersey spiders his way along the chest-high chainlink fence surrounding the basin, trying not to let his feet touch the ground. More people jostle for their turn, posing in front of the water that falls on the opposite side. I'm able to squeeze between a woman in a nylon raspberry sweat suit and a man fixed on his digital camcorder. Less smug than my car, I merely clear my throat.

For as religiously as I watched *Twin Peaks,* my memory of it is actually pretty murky. I remember the weird lighting and crushing on Billy Zane. I remember how the music used to make me feel all geeky and spooked. But in looking at the falls, I think it's also possible that for as much as I liked the series, I might have liked the idea of liking it more. Because the Snoqualmie Falls are good as falls go—the columns of rushing white water are awfully pretty and make that nice crushing sound that waterfalls make—and I definitely recognize them. Looking at them feels like the time I waited on Willem Dafoe: I feel as if we go back, as if we have a friend or bar in common, and I kind of want to stare. Mostly, though, the falls just make me miss the soundtrack. It reminds me that for as conspicuously as I talked about *Twin Peaks*, I never did know what was going on. The same year I rented *Blue Velvet*. I never made it all the way through.

The Broncos kid has made his way to my part of the fence, now followed by his younger sister. Pushing past me, he misses his foothold and falls back on my leg. In lieu of an apology, he brags to his sister that he's still safe because he stepped on me, not the ground. I look at the kid, considering how I could knee him so it looks accidental. Better if there were a way I could take out the guy next to me with the camcorder at the same time. Oblivious to everything outside his camera's peripheral vision, he keeps ramming me with his bag. I watch him lean over the fence and into me, angling his camera away from the crowds and pavement. Other photographers do the same, trying to find a shot where the falls look remote. I take a clue from the kid and step on his foot.

"Oh, I'm so sorry," I lie. He looks annoyed acknowledging me.

At this point, the comparison is moot. Twin Peaks was a small isolated backwoods town. Snoqualmie, I learn from its brochure, is the second most-visited tourist site in Washington. And yet while it seems silly to bemoan this, or to do as the photographers do and try to divorce the experience of seeing the falls from the one of seeing it with hundreds of other people, I'm not above it either.

I stare at the falls.

I watch the water trip on itself, its crash at the bottom, all white and furious.

I watch for a long five or so minutes, determined to have my moment.

Really, though, there is only so much water one can watch fall before the novelty wears out. Then I follow the others to the gift shop. Perhaps buying something will make me feel more profound. I opt for a pretzel at the snack stand, and when the girl at the counter asks if I want salt, I say just a little.

"There was this guy—was it two years or three summers back?—this guy bought a pretzel and he asked for salt on both sides." Her voice rises a few octaves. "Can you believe it?!"

In Twin Peaks, that pretzel might have been the mark of some cattleman's fetish: a normal enough guy who engaged in community events and had a popular daughter, but who would creep into his pasture at night to lap at the salt licks that dotted his farm. In Snoqualmie, however, this pretzel bodes the opposite: that this place is so insipidly predictable that someone asking for extra salt is memorable.

■■■■■■■■■■

I'm beginning to worry a bit about this whole trip of mine. I mean, if I were a *Peaks* Freak and I came here as part of a spiritual pilgrimage, being here might provide some intense emotional fulfillment. I could do all the Lynchian drugs I never did back then and play the soundtrack and wig out on how the owls really weren't what they seem. Maybe I'd still be disappointed. But then it'd at least make sense, the crushing truth of *Twin Peaks*'s nonexistence finally driven home. On the other hand, if I didn't care at all and stopped in Snoqualmie just 'cause, then maybe I'd see it for what it is, treating its televised past with my generation's proper blasé.

Instead, I'm in limbo. As pseudo-into *Twin Peaks* as I was, the fact that I'm weirdly betrayed by its filming sites shows part of me still takes it seriously. I feel stodgy. My mood is dank. No, whatever relationship I have with these sites is a torturous, half-assed one. Worse, the glimpse of its romantic fulfillment that should appear in scene two is nowhere in sight. Right now, I see only continual disappointment.

My current surroundings are another case in point. I sit at the counter in my second *Twin Peaks* location, North Bend's Twedes Café, a.k.a. the R&R Diner, the quiet, unassuming diner where Twin Peaks's Agent Cooper would sit at the counter, order cherry pie, and compliment the coffee as "damn fine, and hot."

It looks, however, like Romper Room. Computerized poker games flash, two televisions run their "look here" advertisements, loudly dressed tourists wave at waitresses from their shiny vinyl seats, and the café's décor is a hideous case of primary colors gone wrong. The window frames are red, the doors are yellow, and those vinyl seats are a shiny blue. The jukebox, the stools: red, yellow, and blue. Even the ceiling, decorated with 1980s neon circles and squares, is in those solid, overstimulating colors. The only signs of the R&R are in the obnoxious, un-*Peaks*-y slogans that splash across the menus, the exterior walls, the waiters' T-shirts, and the bags of coffee beans sold at the register: CHERRY PIE AND A DAMN FINE CUP OF COFFEE. On the back of the waitresses' shirts is more marketed quirk: FOOD SO GREAT, YOU'LL SCRAPE YOUR PLATE. Kyle MacLachlan would cringe.

I sit at the counter, waiting for a cup of chili. It's been thirty-eight minutes. All of the waitresses are too busy to talk, and I see no hunched-over regular whose mumbled barbs will reveal North Bend for what it really is. So I sit by myself, committing Twedes's menu to memory. It tells of a fire in 2000 that led to the diner's remodeled decor. It also summarizes the history of the Snoqualmie area, beginning with the arrival of the first permanent white settler and climaxing with the arrival of David Lynch. Every sentence about *Twin Peaks* ends with an exclamation point, my least favorite punctuation mark. Between readings, I perfect my pie order: "Yeah, a slice of pie sounds good. What kind do you have?" I'll opt for cherry as if it's a coincidence and slip in an order of decaf like an afterthought.

This is bad. Really, I mortify myself. I'm such a dork. And not in the unique, interesting way *Twin Peaks* celebrated. Not even in the passionate, geeked-out way those *Peaks* Freaks are. I look through the tourist thicket, searching out someone to make fun of to make me feel better. In the kitchen, one of the line cooks has a three-inch green Mohawk. It's a brave color to sport in this despotic color scheme. It's also the only vaguely Native American thing I've seen in all of Snoqualmie Valley. Other than that, everyone looks the same. Perhaps underneath their tourist outfits many of my fellow diners are legitimate oddballs and freaks, but from here, they all look the same.

No, I'm a dork in that horrible high school, thinking I can be different from them because of the way I order my dessert.

After forty-two minutes, my waitress at last delivers my chili.

"Busy, eh?" I try.

"It's okay." She drops the check before I can even ask for the pie.

So I sit, eating my chili. It's not even hot. I should just go ahead and ask for the damn pie and coffee, but my self-consciousness cripples me. I put down a five and get out.

■ ■ ■ ■ ■ ■ ■ ■ ■

Outside North Bend, low clouds darken the sky. Fog tethers against the mountains, obscuring their height, and shades all but the closest trees gray. I drive, listening to the rumble of tires and pavement, glad for the muted colors. It's good to be back in my car. It's easier to like myself here. I follow the road north and east, past an Irish pasture, a rocky creek. I listen to the road and when I'm over that, I put on some moody ballads. It works as if on cue. I no longer feel like shit. I'm just melancholy.

I stop for gas at a nameless exit, scrub insects off my window and chat weather with the old attendant who insists on pumping my gas. I'm back on the road, and the trees and gray grow thicker. One of my safety precautions for my trip was a dashboard compass. It's a cheap plastic gizmo with Old World letters. I watch its needle quiver about the E. So far I've been on a familiar coast, safely within reach of homes I know. Headed into the country, I feel as if I'm at last really leaving. Leaving the Pacific, leaving its comfort, maybe even leaving the awkwardness and ineptness and annoying restraint that have so far kept me company.

I'm on my own now. I'm surprised to find it a relief.

I continue east for more than an hour, past more gorgeous meetings of tree, rock, and river until I reach the turnoff for Roslyn. It leads me to a narrow, curving road through woodland. A few miles more and there it is: that wide, instantly recognizable street, looking just as it should. On the right is the KBHR radio station. On the left, The Brick bar. They make me a little giddy. Across the street I spot the general store, and farther down is the Roslyn Café mural. Many of the buildings and signs used in the show are still here. I see The Brick and the Sodylicious Café, the Northwestern Mining buildings, and a store with the white letters DR. JOEL FLEISHMAN scrawled on its windowpane. The place where Chris, the heady DJ and *Northern Exposure*'s spiritual narrator, waxed poetic looks as if he just left it. I peek in the window and see the faded postcards on the wall and the records strewn, untouched, as in the bedroom of a dead child.

Of course, a number of things are here that wouldn't belong in Cicely, the small, fictional Alaskan town where a Jewish New York doctor worked on medical assignment. The community is larger than in *Northern Exposure*. Neighborhoods and businesses stretch well beyond its famous two blocks. New-model cars line the street, people mill about taking pictures, and placards dot the sidewalk: RUTH-ANNE'S GENERAL STORE AS SEEN ON NE. Like Twin Peaks, Cicely was home to an array of characters—a recovering Valley girl, a Native shaman, a right-wing ex-astronaut, a female pilot whose boyfriends died in freak accidents—many of whom now pose in the town's photos and post-cards. Walking around, I think it's a little weird to be in a town that is perpetually paying tribute to a fictional version of itself, but then again, the absurdity suits it. The street has a lazy vibe, and Labor Day feels instantly less laborious.

As magical as it was, though, Cicely also seemed equally ordinary. Unlike the Aaron Spelling series of its time, *Northern Exposure* had normal-looking folks wearing winter jackets and comfortable shoes. In Cicely, there was a certain physical plausibility, which perhaps made me willing to believe the rest of it could be real, too. I stroll down the street, still aware of how long I linger at television landmarks, running a tally of which things here are not like the other. The random sundries in the general store: quirky. The swanky restaurant next door: not. Someone has ridden a horse into town that waits in a parking spot. Tourists snap its photo: so very Cicely. The drive-through espresso stand, the young people loitering about: not. And when I have a seat in the Roslyn Café, I quickly ascribe the handwritten, grammatically unconventional sign by my table to the quirky column.

> *During our busy times we can take up to 50 minutes to get your meal out to you. We have only a 4 foot grill and it holds only 8 burger or sandwiches and all the fixings for each item. We have two cooks and a back up person plus several others persons to run for us. Your waitress puts the time on each ticket when she put it in to us and they are taken in the order they come to us. Please be patient—it is not your waitresses fault for your meal to take so long. — Karen*

I much prefer the sign to Twedes's T-shirts, though I'm torn over which of my impulses is worse—to jot Karen a quick edit or be patronizingly charmed. I settle for scolding both my temptations and, when the waitress approaches, order a slice of pie, cherry.

■ ■■ ■■ ■■ ■■ ■

I returned to Roslyn after a detour into nearby Cle Elum, a low, wide town that made up for its lack of architectural charm with an abundance of cheap motels. I got a room and killed some time with the Discovery Channel. Then I groomed until I felt obligated to go out. I put on my tight Carson City Hot Springs T, mascara, and boots and, fighting every desire to stay in and watch the next *Shark Week* special, drove back to Roslyn. *Northern Exposure* offered a lesson: No one in Cicely ever did anything half-assed. If I wanted to know Roslyn apart from the show, I needed to do better than just keep score. Plus, earlier in the day, I had seen a sign for live music at The Brick, Cicely's local bar. I figured watching music would make my evening rituals a little easier. It'd give me an activity to excuse my solitude.

And when I entered The Brick, I thought it just might work. It gave me the same flush of comfort the town did when I first saw it. Dimly lit, with high ceilings and a dark wood ornate bar, the bar had a couple of video games and pool tables in the back and a requisite elk head over the door. A server with a high blond ponytail and bubble gum–pink nails looked like *Northern Exposure*'s Shelly reincarnate. Both roomy and cozy, The Brick reminded me of a big friend from back home, a bear of a guy who hugs me hard and long.

Only, I'd read the sign wrong. There is no music tonight, just

SCHULER BOOKS
&MUSIC

Schuler Books and Music

1982 Grand River Avenue
Okemos, MI
(517) 349-8840   (800) 347-8841

STORE: 0024   REG: 02/55   TRAN#: 8796
SALE   07/21/2010   EMP: 00211

SCHULER REMAINDE
  000666661973   SR T   1.99
      3.99 50%PROMOTION

              Subtotal   1.99
              MICHIGAN 6%   .12
  1 Item   Total   2.11
              CASH   3.00
              Cash Change Due .89

You Saved $2.00

      07/21/2010 01:09PM

Mon-Sat 9 am - 9 pm
Sunday 11 am - 6 pm
Returns within 30 days with receipt
CDs and DVDs must be unopened
Used books are not returnable

a couple of college-age kids playing games in the back, a row of guys at the bar, and Bill.

"I'd love to show you some local places. I mean, you're a very attractive woman. . . . What's your name again? There's this great swimming hole. I also know a great place for breakfast."

Bill is in his thirties—tall, lean, and wearing carpenter jeans and a T-shirt. His brown hair tufts out the bottom of his baseball cap and he's working on a goatee. His eyes have a sailor's squint.

"I mean, I'm not trying to be fresh or anything, but you're very pretty and you're not gonna meet many guys with two-hundred-year-old antiques. You should really come over and check 'em out. . . . I'm sorry, but did you tell me your name?"

Bill isn't unattractive, and were he less focused on getting me in bed and more on remembering my name, he might even be cute. I ignore his come-ons and ask him about Roslyn.

"Ah, I like it all right. Changed a lot, but still damn beautiful." He shifts back in his stool. "The winters, though, are something else. I was seeing this girl from Seattle—she was thirteen years younger than me—but she couldn't handle it. Said the eight feet of snow was seven feet too much for her."

Bill has a habit of doing this—slipping in informational footnotes that he thinks will increase his sex appeal. He talks about his carpentry ("So, you know I'm good with my hands") and how his ex-wife was an Eddie Bauer fashion designer, which means—he says with peculiar confidence—he has nice suits. In case a pair of quality slacks doesn't seal the deal, he also makes sure I have enough beer, nodding the bartender my way even though my glass is half full.

"Don't worry," he says, resting his hand on my back, "I'll take care of you."

"Oh, I can do that myself, thanks."

Bill recognizes no reproach. Nor does he notice when I turn from him to a nearby picture board tacked with photos. The same faces wear sloppy grins in front of seasonal bar decor: shamrocks, pumpkins, and Christmas lights. I nod as Bill tells me about his hot tub, still scanning the photos for people on the Cicely side of my scoreboard. Instead they look a lot like the people I pegged for tourists around me: young, similar, altogether ordinary.

Bill keeps talking. I push back my stool. Bill tries one more invitation.

"Before you go, let me at least take you to Marco's. It's like the real Brick." He smiles and squints. He does it well: "It's where people from Roslyn really go."

■ ■ ■ ■ ■ ■ ■ ■ ■ ■

Outside, mist thickens Roslyn's main strip. A few cars hunker below the streetlights. My boots sound obnoxious in the quiet. We walk up the unfilmed blocks to where a Budweiser sign colors the fog red.

Bill turns to me seriously: "I'm sorry. I want to introduce you to some friends in here, but I think I've forgotten your name."

No, his mind isn't exactly a steel trap, but neither does he strike me as a bad guy.

Bill opens the door and leads me into Marco's. It has twice as many customers as The Brick, Outkast blares in the back, and peanut shells crunch underfoot. A brown dog makes rounds, enjoying pets at each table he greets. Above the door, instead of an elk head, there is the head of an antlered rabbit. I hang back while Bill makes the rounds. I watch people give me the once- and twice-overs and am grateful when Bill introduces me around.

The female bartender has a hard grip and a strong voice as she introduces this place with a comparison to *Cheers:* "Everyone knows your goddamn name, whether you want them to or not." She passes me on to Fred, warning me he is "on vacation." A slight truck driver with long gray hair and heavy lids, Fred jiggles my hand as if he were trying to shake it loose. He tells me about flying and music, assuring me that he has "an affinity with female rockers" and that he feels "the Allman Brothers hard." Fred invites me to a game of pool and I'm at my two-and-a-half-beer best. I nail a tough bank shot and ignore the "shark" comments as if it were nothing.

"So, you from here?" I ask Fred as I pocket the eight.

"Awww, no. About as many natives here as there are jackelope."

His head lolls toward the antlered rabbit. "But I've been 'round long 'nough. Top-notch town. I'll tell you that."

"How's that vacation going, Fred?" Bill checks in.

"Rockin', my man. I'm rockin'." Fred closes his eyes and leans against the wall.

"How about you, doll?" Bill says, finding a way around his amnesia problem. He eases Fred's stick from his hands. "Everyone treating you right?"

I smile, aware he mistakes my good mood for interest. "You dare take me on?"

He wins the first game. Lets me take the second. And I'm liking Roslyn. It may not be as diverse as Cicely, but it's got its characters. I sit out a couple of games to chat with the bartender and pet the dog. Another hour and another beer, I've even stopped making comparisons. I don't notice until something makes me start again.

After a round of doubles, Bill's returned to his favorite topics of conversation. I'm leaning over, aiming the six-ball in the side pocket, and he's telling me about his antiques and that I'm attractive when I notice several girls looking at me. When our eyes meet, they turn toward each other and one moves her head as if she is discussing something, or rather someone, she doesn't like. I move away from Bill and try the shot from another angle. I sink a solid and scratch the white.

The girls' scrutiny sobers me. Self-conscious, I look around.

One woman drapes herself over her date. A guy veers heavy-footed to the bathroom. Bill asks my name again and tells me a story about his younger girlfriend he has told me four times. I no longer pretend I haven't heard it already. Suddenly, the way Bill talks, it reminds me of the Snoqualmie girl telling me about the pretzel. He speaks of it with wow, with exclamation points.

In Cicely, the doctor's secretary, Marilyn, would deliver information on a patient's attempt to fly with the same deadpan she announced the time. A stranger would enter The Brick and barely be noticed. In Cicely, people didn't pass judgment on random acts of art, gossip about age differences, or get routinely drunk at the neighborhood bar. Instead, everything and everyone was accepted with an unquestioning aplomb. I never thought about it at the time, but from the pool table at Marco's, Cicely's wildest quirk was not in its stories or characters, but in its immunity to the pedestrian details of real small-town life. It might have looked more normal than Melrose Place, but the fact that Cicely was a remote town where few grew bored, got smashed, gossiped, felt trapped, or were skeptical of a stranger now seems just as fantastical.

By now, Bill has all but won the game. He's got one ball to my three and an easy corner shot. Pocketing the last solid, he belatedly asks me if I'm in a relationship. I tell him I'm not and ask him the same question back. He says "kinda," an interesting word choice that I find means he has a girlfriend of four years. Tired from the wedding they attended this weekend, she stayed home tonight.

Bill sinks the eight and it's time for me to go. I try to leave on my own but Bill insists on walking me back. At my car, he says goodbye and wishes me luck like a perfect gentleman. I look back at Roslyn in my rearview mirror. It's dark and still and even leaves me satisfied.

INTERSTATE 90, WASHINGTON

The next morning, I continue east across Washington. Midway through, I stop. The air is hot, the wind is dry, and the fields look like sand dunes, rolling and stretching in straw blond. Here and there are the darker clumps of shrubs and rocks, but they too are blanched light. Through this prairie desert cuts the Columbia River Gorge. The walls of the river rise, carved with grooves. The Columbia looks still between them.

While I was fighting against wind and semis, the road into this scene felt fat and hard, but from where I stand now, the interstate is only a line in the sand. I've stopped on the site of something significant, though I'm at a loss for what. The informational plaques in the vista parking lot have been pried off and replaced with graffiti, pedestals for the initials of Been Heres. The wind blows the road noise quiet and on the hillside behind me, the copper statues of fourteen wild horses pose like freedom.

Sitting on my hood, I watch an RV take the looping

road off the freeway to the vista. The RV pulls next to me and a couple steps down from their cab, twisting their torsos, shaking their legs. We exchange pleasantries.

"What brings you out this way by yourself?"

I give them an abbreviated story. The woman asks me, "All by yourself? How do your parents feel about this? If I were your mom, I wouldn't have let you go."

I answer with a smile and ask if they wouldn't mind taking my picture. I grin for the camera, hair awry, wearing Sears overalls that make me look less than my age. I wear some remainder makeup from going out in Roslyn the night before and a tan from the two weeks on the road. I look girly. I feel happy.

Somewhere back in California, I met a young guy named Aaron. Aaron was lean, taut with muscles, and some part of his body was always twitching in anticipation. He moved like a dog being teased with a tennis ball. Aaron was on the onset of the Great American Road Trip, though he was doing it the "right" way: a couple hundred bucks, no car, no reservations, no expectations. He was going to hitchhike and bus his way around the United States and see where he ended up.

"Yeah, I'm just going where the road takes me," he said, scratching his stomach, tapping his heel. "I've left it all behind."

After some time talking, comparing the overly structured nature of my trip with the perfect spontaneity of his, Aaron told me he knew of this hidden beach on the coast. He let me know he was an Aries, which, incidentally, meant he was a very good lover. I didn't doubt him. He looked to have the energy of his nineteen years. But I somehow suspect he wouldn't have told me that if I were the single, nomadic guy he was.

I'm 5'5", with blondish curly hair and a curvy figure. My build is sturdy but fit, and I have a look that some call exotic, though that might just be a euphemism for having big hair, big eyes, and big breasts. I know being a young woman has its advantages. I know my appearance has garnered me introductions I would've otherwise had to work for. Middle-aged men greet me with smiles. Older women welcome me with "honeys" and "dears."

But I didn't follow Aaron to the beach. Partly because he looked a bit too much like a Labrador for me to take him seriously, but also because for as unthreatening as he was, and as strong as I personally feel, being a woman, I don't feel the luxury of Aaron's young, male, invulnerable abandon. I'm female and I'm alone. I can't leave these things behind.

"I hope you have a safe trip, dear," the woman says as her husband hands me back my camera. "And be careful."

I thank them and turn my camera to the horses. Three of the statues lead the pack out to a view of the Columbia. They are midgallop, front legs reaching out, manes windblown back. A trail leads up to where they stand and I follow it. The path is dusty and steep and, ultimately, disillusioning. Up close, the horses look much less majestic. Their metal slabs are flat, rusted, and marked with graffiti. They look less free than melded stiff.

The horses do, however, provide some coverage for a needed bathroom break. Careful that my feet are not downstream, I squat on the slope behind the statues. The arid ground lacks absorbency. Pee splashes back at my thighs. So I stay there: crouched, overalls around my ankles, air-drying. My gender may have its advantages. This is not one of them.

CHAPTER THREE

A River Runs Through It

"Eventually, all things merge into one,
and a river runs through it."

[NORMAN, A RIVER RUNS THROUGH IT]

"Don't worry," Bob Marley sings, "'bout a thing." Bob is performing live and I've got the whole stoned stadium urging him on through my speakers.

"Every little thing gonna be all right," he continues, and I'm almost inclined to believe him. Only it's not the little things I'm currently concerned with. It's the big ones. Speeding trucks on blind corners. Falling rocks. Being completely lost, running out of gas, being mauled by a grizzly, and having the scraps of my flesh float downstream, feeding the salmon spawn of St. Joe River. What's worse, I don't even know what state is going to sign off my death certificate. I think I'm heading east but am not too sure, and while my survival skills are admittedly feeble, I'm not keen on their failing me in Idaho. If I succumb to a long and unpleasant death, I'd rather do it in Big Sky Country than in the Land of Famous Potatoes. The latter just sounds as pathetic as I feel.

This road I'm on seemed initially a dandy idea. Too many hours on the interstate convinced me to get off it. My attention kept pushing ahead of where I was; I felt I was losing some sort of race. The road map showed a gray line that paralleled I-90's blue stripe through Idaho's panhandle before it met back with the freeway in southwest Montana. I decided to take it.

And for the first hour or so, this was a fine plan. Though the path I followed was hardly as focused as the straight line on my map, the land was beautiful and fairly calm. The road wove through a mountain crease, trailing the river's course of least resistance. Hills of pine sloped up at reasonable angles, and every few miles pickup trucks parked in pullouts, men dressed in beige wading in the water nearby. The river itself was also well mannered. Its gray water occasionally hit rock and tickled white, but for the most part, the river didn't run through the mountains as much as it meandered in between.

That has since changed. In the two hours I've been driving, the road and its surroundings have grown increasingly aggressive. Yellow signs warn where erosion and falling rocks squeeze the asphalt's two lanes to one. The road's crimps swing into wider curves, the pine slants steeper, and the sky has darkened to the color of smudged charcoal. Which would still be fine if I were sure I was on the right road and/or headed in the right direction. I've been on this road far longer than that benign gray line indicates and am no closer to anything resembling civilization.

The problem, of course, is that I've stumbled onto the altogether wrong set. I'm headed toward Montana, not for *Deliverance*—it's not on my schedule for another couple of months—but for Robert Redford's *A River Runs Through It,* the 1992 movie based on Norman Maclean's memoir about his youth in Missoula in the early twentieth century, fly-fishing with his brother on Big Blackfoot River. The movie in which Brad Pitt played his signature role—the wild, well-abbed bad boy—and Montana played hers: big mountains, long expanses, open space, and that infamous sky. Even upon second and third viewings, long after my *Thelma and Louise* Pitt crush faded, *River*'s portrait still moves me. In it, Montana is the anticity. The real Wild West. The state for Man to battle land and animal, confront death, and reckon with that from which he came.

Only that's Montana, and I'm not there yet, I don't think, and am thus quite unprepared to battle nature or to commune with earth.

Instead, I'm crowded on this decaying road in Idaho, a state better known for starch crops and racist enclaves.

So, rather than getting in touch with the great outdoors, I'm connecting with the assorted technology I have inside my car.

Besides the laptop, cell phone, and camera, I have a mini tape recorder on the dashboard, a CD player on the passenger seat, and Bob Marley on the stereo, singing of a place far away from bears and fast water. I play it loud, hoping the crowds will distract me from my decreasing gas tank and inspire a celebration I can't seem to muster on my own. The only times I lower the radio are when I try to talk myself down with my tape recorder. I make myself note just how the rocks bare themselves, the marvelously ominous colors of the encroaching sky. Yes, I say, the river sure is striking now that it's tight and studded with granite edges. It helps to hear that humming whirl of the recorder as an external recognition I exist, especially seeing as this is a condition that's soon to change.

Another hour of driving and it's official: I'm really fucking nervous. The pickups have disappeared and the road is under outright attack. The river takes increasingly frequent bites out of the asphalt, and the mountain's rocks seem determined to cover it up. The sky keeps lowering like a *Temple of Doom* booby trap—a crack of thunder the exact sound of the crushing skull Indy uses to try to stop it—and I swear I just saw the river flash its teeth.

What's more, those quaint yellow warnings of the narrowing road have been forsaken altogether. Heading into a blind curve, the pavement will suddenly slip into the river or under the mountain, and it's up to me to avoid whatever natural or sixteen-wheeled obstacle comes my way. I turn up Bob another notch and rest a little heavier on the gas pedal. Blind corners be damned, I want this drive to end. It may be smarter to drive slowly, but my mind is too busy imagining gory, lingering deaths to deal with something as petty as safety.

I eventually see a road sign, and a bit of my heart jumps at the sighting of human language. What it says, however, is considerably less comforting:

WARNING. UNMAINTAINED ROAD AHEAD.

The asphalt steers away from the river and climbs into the mountains. Contrary to the sign's warning, the road is actually better than the river route, and the improved conditions make me think this road meets up with a freeway after all. The forest is less daunting when it's not just above me. The higher vistas give me hope that a view of civilization awaits me on top. I drive up the mountain, my optimism rising with the elevation. *Maybe those aren't dark clouds of death. Maybe they just carry rain. Surely, there are fewer grizzlies in those mountains than there are jackrabbits and songbirds.* By the time I reach the summit, I've almost got myself feeling cheerful. Except it's then I see that rather than any Arcos or comforting man-made things on the horizon, there is nothing but trees.

All around me, mountain after monotonous mountain, is a cruel carpet of green.

And up ahead, the road turns to gravel. *Shit. This is so not okay.*

I'm too far along now; I could never make it back with the gas I have. So, going far too fast in neutral to save fuel, I continue down the mountain. I drive in the middle of the road, partly so that when the gravel shifts under me, I have room to slide, and partly for the visual buffer of having man's work on either side of me. Even Marley is no help now. The crowd's enthusiasm sounds like a taunt. I drive for what feels like days in silence.

The patches of visible sky darken to a deeper blue. The mountain is shrouded in shadow. At one point, I see a weathered roadwork sign—FLAGGER AHEAD—but miles pass with no sight of him. More miles, another orange sign, and still no sign of humans; my paranoia peaks. Obviously, this means the flagger's been offed and no one's even bothered to notice his absence. I wonder what did him in. A bear? A backwoodsman? Or more likely, Wilderness itself. A conspiracy of River, Forest, and Rock.

Then I see it: a flash of orange.

It's moving. And it's a girl at that.

As I approach, she puts down her walkie-talkie. By the size of my smile, she must think I'm having an obscenely good time.

"It'll be just a moment. The helicopter's just finishing loading the logs." Then, before I can even ask, her walkie-talkie sputters static and she waves me along. "The freeway's not fifteen minutes ahead. Enjoy Montana."

■■■■■■■■■

At this point, it's not much of a revelation when I confess I'm not a big outdoorswoman. I mean, I've camped on occasion, but Brad, or at least he as Montana's ultimate nature boy (a role he reprised in the similar though awful *Legends of the Fall*) would never fall for the likes of me. In the city/country dichotomy, I fall firmly on the former side. My time with the great outdoors is usually limited to runs around Oakland's man-made Lake Merritt. My closet contains no fleece. My wilderness skills—I did once whittle a walking stick—couldn't save me from a squirrel.

Being a city girl, I also think that when it comes to movies such as *A River Runs Through It*, I'm more credulous. Gimme a chick flick and I'll rip it from start to finish, but I don't have much personal know-how about father-son relationships, male bonding, or fishing; I'm more likely to take *River*'s version of these things at face value. Redford's direction might've been heavy-handed. The Big Blackfoot comes off as transcendental. Maclean's brother is like a Greek fishing god. But who am I to say it's too romantic or nostalgic? Maybe that's just the way fishing in Montana is.

After a night in a hotel off the freeway, trying to ready myself for

Montana by watching local cable hunting shows, I consult my maps for a route toward where *River* was filmed. When Maclean was growing up in Missoula, it was a small town newly accessible by railroad. Now Missoula is Montana's second-largest city, complete with a university and some tall buildings that beckon to me from the freeway.

Alas, this Missoula isn't the Montana of the movie. Because of Missoula's growth, *A River Runs Through It*'s city scenes were shot in the smaller towns to the east, Bozeman and Livingston. Even the Big Blackfoot of the movie is not the real Big Blackfoot. Development and logistics required Redford to film on other rivers to the south and east. This kind of dislocation complicates my trip. I say I want to see the real Missoula, but what I really want to see is the place I think of as Missoula. Thus, instead of visiting the places as they are named, and though it pains me to think of all the good cafés and college radio stations I'm leaving behind, I continue past Missoula. Instead, I've resolved to go to the places that have formed my images. So to Bozeman I go. Getting there necessitates driving more freeway, many parts of which are remarkably ugly. The sky is in all sorts of indecision, the low mountains of dry grass are drab, and sparse trees stick from them like bad transplants.

I am still skeptical of portraits of America's back roads, mostly for the fact that road flicks show them at all. If a pair were trying to get cross-country fast—and most road protagonists are in some sort of hurry—they probably wouldn't opt for the two-lane scenic route. Yet I have to admit that, Idaho's aside, the smaller roads are winning me over. I spot a detour on the way to Bozeman, relaxing the minute I'm on it. As I loop south by ranch gates, cows, and pasture, the land that looked underdressed from the interstate suddenly feels downright sexy. The land's scarcity now seems spacious, the sky's uncertainty exciting. A man on a horse tips his brim my direction and I actually let out a moan.

Shortly thereafter, I reach a vista where I can see a distant mountain range. The surrounding fields are flat and gold. The mountains do their thing, overlapping in receding shades of blue, and just above the white-capped peaks is the most well-placed tuft of clouds. It's as perfect as a printed check. On this, I think the movies don't lie. Montana's not just photogenic, it's breathtaking. I could almost pull over, pledge myself to it, forsake my urban ways. Instead I opt to savor the view over a cup of coffee in a lone nearby diner. I take one sip of the rehydrated crystals while listening to a twangy song on the radio. Any thoughts of my country conversion are mercifully killed.

■■■■■■■■■■

It's said that Montana has a split through it. This divide used to be referred to as the Old and New Wests: the Old counties having an older working class of ranchers, miners, and farmers, the New having more college-educated professionals and service workers, increased tourism, and a growing population. Eastern Montana—arid and sparse—

represents much of the Old, while Bozeman, which grew 4 percent a year in the early nineties, is often cited as the model of the New. A study after the last Montana census renamed these Old and New West counties with more appropriate titles: Cowboy and Cappuccino. In Montana, it seems, there's an inverse ratio between one's coffee and one's masculinity. Where the coffee is strong, the men are soft, and thus Missoula and Bozeman, with their art galleries and poetry readings, are said to be in cappuccino counties.

This can make for abrupt transitions. I can't find the exact locations of *River*'s filming sites in Bozeman, so I stroll its streets, eyeing anything familiar. I pass buildings' century-old facades, others all mirror and glass. Cowboy hats top the heads of both old men, on whom they look an innate part of the face, and young women, who pair them with sandals.

At one point, looking for a lead, I stop in a sporting goods store that must get great insulation from the number of animals mounted on its walls: elks, goats, rabbits, lacquered fish, five whole moose, and three bears, as well as mounted bear heads, paws, and roaring throw rugs. It reminds me of the bear-hunting show I saw the other night, the majority of which consisted of a guy sitting in a tree house in front of a large barrel of raw meat, eating pumpkin seeds and skimming through a magazine. His only stealth came the moment he belatedly heard a bear rummaging through his trap and had to put down his snacks without wrinkling the plastic and, with no more apparent skill than it takes to work an unfamiliar remote control, put a bullet in the fleeing bear. The bears around me are all staged in the most menacing positions. Maybe if Redford had directed the show, cutting out a few of the snacking scenes, taping some postproduction shots of the hunter pontificating into the distance, this place would promise some *River*-ish spiritual connection to nature. As is, it leaves me cold.

Down the street, I try the Bozeman Angler shop. It is to the first sporting goods store what World Wrestling Entertainment is to cricket. Its walls are painted shades of tan and rows of pocketed vests hang well pressed. It looks like Pottery Barn. The people working the shop wear their cotton Ts as if they were linen, and though they are excessively friendly—they struggle to think of Bozeman filming sites, and when I ask them if they know anywhere I can watch the U.S. Open tennis finals, they go so far as to call some of the sports bars in town—their shop doesn't seem like *River*'s nature, either. Its rods and pretty books remind me not of the movie's fishing scenes, but of the ones with the cousin from Hollywood. Of his white clothes and comic pretensions. Everything is so clean and expensive and nice, it'd seem a shame to get them wet.

It's hardly novel, this mix that's Montana. Played out under the names of gentrification or development, the conflict between an old culture and a new economy, between country life and city influx, is at the root of most identity struggles. I've seen it everywhere I've been yet. But if the conflict is complex—a debate of economy and culture, nostalgia and growth—it doesn't often feel that way. It often feels as simple as two sides, with little doubt about who is in the right.

Watch any movie. The signifiers are so often the same: The good guy wears worn jeans, the evil one talks on his cell and orders coffee with too many modifiers. In pop culture, the city folk are silly, affected, and disconnected from the basics. Like that Hollywood cousin. And while *River's* narrator is hardly a bad character, his urban habits surely are: his name-dropping, his conservative drinking, his city-sloppy casts. "The city has softened you, big brother," Brad says, his skin sun kissed, his hair wild. This is obviously not a good thing.

Walking out of the angler shop, I skim an article in the local paper about the census: "If the trends continue, the Old West may become increasingly isolated . . . as urbanites and their 'cappuccino' counterparts in the Rural West join forces."

I didn't think I came here as part of some urbanite force. I don't consider myself the bad guy. That said, I do like my coffee hard and my nature weak. Nearby is a café and I head toward it. Several Harley clichés lean against their bikes outside. One shoots me a smile and, still hoping to bond with others over sport, I ask if he knows anywhere playing the Open. They look at me as if I have a toy poodle in tow.

"Baby, we don't watch that kind of stuff around here," says one. He has ample facial growth, a spherical belly, and a collage of tattoos.

"You can watch it from my place," suggests his friend, lifting his eyebrows for extra effect. His outfit is as subtle as his approach. The back of his shirt reads: IF YOU CAN READ THIS, THE BITCH FELL OFF.

I turn back to the first guy: "Is it sissy?"

"No, baby," he replies with kind restraint, "people just have different tastes."

■■■■■■■■■

The next day, after watching the Open in my motel room—a match between the Williams sisters, in which I saw more black people than I've seen in all of the last two states—I move on to Livingston, where supposedly the majority of *River* was filmed. Moving east from Missoula to Bozeman to Livingston feels like working on increasingly worn-in knee pads. By the time I get to Livingston, I can feel through the cushion to the bone. Much of this is due to a combination of valley stretches, river corridors, and mountain passes that funnel wind through Livingston with tidal force. The wind catches my car's canvas like a sail. I have to muscle my steering wheel to keep it on the road.

Livingston is also where the cowboys officially regain their reins. Agriculture remains the primary economy. The lumber mill is still functional. This doesn't mean the town is destitute—gift shops are tucked among the storefronts and espresso is widely available— but Livingston lacks Bozeman's cuteness. The streets are wide and dry, the downtown a gulf. Much of Livingston is lost in the vastness of land and sky. It feels temporary, as if time could slip it elsewhere. It acts as if it's under threat, as if the wind is just biding its time before it blows it away.

The same combination of landscape that blesses the town with such terrific winds, however, also helps it enjoy advantages over many of its cowboy cousins. It hasn't experienced Bozeman's boom, but Livingston has developed steadily during the last ten years. Its proximity to Yellowstone National Park has provided it with increasing tourism, and its varied scenery has helped it land many film roles. Go into the local museum and you can see evidence of those films and the actors who've bought land in the area. Peter Fonda is a neighbor, and his Captain America jacket from *Easy Rider* sits in a Plexiglas display. Robert Redford filmed both *River* and *The Horse Whisperer* in Livingston, contributing to both the local image and the museum's memorabilia.

Yet even the glitterati match the town, they being weathered, taciturn men. And so would the place seem to fit their fame. It has to be easier to be recognizable in a place where no one is anonymous. Such is Livingston. Eating out at a diner, every male wears a hat and the waitress greets every customer by name.

Well, everyone but me.

I miss Bozeman's camouflage. College kids. Tourists. Nothing in Livingston is any more familiar. Only here, my solitude, my gender, and my cityness seem magnified. One night I go out in my jeans, boots, and thrift-store Western shirt. I've never felt like a more horrible poseur. I feel like a fly, and not the kind that goes unnoticed on a wall, but the kind peddled in the angler shop: an outrageous assortment of hook and feather that no real insect would ever confuse for its own.

So I go back to donning the good ol' urban armor of feigning I'm fearless and gravitate to the activities where my solitude and strangeness feel like a choice. A run. The museum. Livingston's artsy coffee shop:

"Hunting is beyond dualisms. . . . There's a moment of communion with the animal, when it was perceived not as an object, perhaps not as subject, but as surely beyond that dichotomy." I read this in a book called *A Quiet Place of Violence* in a café that also fits the title. For such a humble town, its coffee shop has a lot of gothic edge. The lighting is minimal and the walls are dark and decorated with very angry art, dirty white backgrounds scrawled with blood-red, monosyllabic words: WHY WORK. LOVE SICK. BAD DOG. DICK HEAD.

"Hunting must be right in that it returns us to the nature from which we evolved, deobjectifying the world. We're no longer watching the world, we're participating in it as essential members." Personally, I could justify my presence in this café with the fact that caffeine is the nature from which I evolved, but I suppose that would be missing the point. If only it weren't so much easier to watch. Above my head is a canvas that reads HOPE LESS. It feels accusatory.

■ ■■■■■■■ ■■

I'm on my way out the next morning when, out of obligation, I stop by Livingston's Fly Fishing Federation. Defeat precedes me. I look around for a while, at the old rods on display, the wicker fishing baskets like the ones used in the movie. Testimonials celebrate fly-fishing with *River's* same spiritual poetry. Maclean's quotes are framed on the wall. It's not that I don't believe them. I get that fishing means a lot to certain people, but without the movie's narrative, their passion doesn't make it mean any more to me.

After a while, the director of the Federation, Matt, introduces himself. He's one of the passionate ones. He spends an hour with me discussing the history of the sport, the museum's education program for schoolchildren, and its catch-and-release policy: "Many of the trout populations are endangered, and we want to make sure that we save this resource for future generations to enjoy." He actually talks like this. It's so civilized, less a battle of life and death with nature than a friendly game of Frisbee.

The Federation has a workshop for making flies, and Matt ties me one. He's also going out to the river after work, as he always does, and invites me along. I tell him I'm moving on to Wyoming. I don't know why. As I leave, he gives me his card. "If you change your mind and feel like fishing, just give me a ring."

I get in my car and leave Livingston. I continue out of town for fifteen minutes before a trail sign makes me pull over. Of course, that was what was so bothersome about the TV's bear hunter: On his perch, he never put himself out there. The battle of Man versus Nature is nothing compared to the battle of man and his own nature.

I search through my bag for Matt's card. My stomach churns as I dial his number. He says to swing by at five. He also recommends the nearby trailhead. Guilt makes me give it a go.

There's a line in *A River Runs Through It*. It's about the father's belief that all things good, whether eternal salvation or trout, come through grace. It follows that grace comes through art and art isn't easy, which is a comfort, because my hiking isn't a very graceful venture.

After packing my Mace and whistle, studying the bear warning signs as if they were a doctor's prescription, and heading up the trail, I realize not only that my weaponry would be more likely to piss off a grizzly than to scare it away, but that in all my planning for bear, I am least prepared for the other nature right in front of me. The last several days have dusted Livingston's peaks white, and within half an hour of hiking, the path is covered in snow. Dressed in loose Levi's and tennis shoes—an outfit better suited for a casual Friday than for scaling a slushy trail—I figure it is an even gamble on which will take my legs first, frostbite or bear bites. Within a couple of miles, my toes are already numb, and though I have no idea what bear footsteps sound like, the plod of dropping snow keeps me alert.

The hike, however, affords some mighty vistas. The brightened ground helps the sun dazzle as if it were not just stuck in the sky. The trees look good in white. At one point near the top, wet to the knees, I get lost in the view of snow and sky and peaks all around. I take a picture I know will not do it justice. I try to think of words that are at all adequate. I am a bit annoyed, having all that emotion and no outlet—like having a mad, unrequited crush—and maybe part of it is due to the altitude, but it fills my chest with ache. After a while, I have to turn away.

On my way down, I come across fellow hikers—two men dressed wisely in boots and Gore-tex—and share a smile of mutual accomplishment, an appreciation for nature's beauty.

"Did you see the bear tracks?" they ask excitedly.

I had suspected that's what those round prints were, but I'd spied them at the onset of my warm, fuzzy, altitude-drunk phase and had convinced myself otherwise. "Oh no, you're not supposed to tell me that."

"I wouldn't worry. They looked old." Except it only snowed this morning.

They wish me well and continue up the mountain, smiling. I continue down it, on my ass. It really was a horrid movie—the ending scene of Brad's being mauled by a bear was so awfully done—still, that *Legends of the Fall* scene runs through my head. Running the now-mud path in bald tennis shoes, I slide my way down, grabbing onto feeble branches, breaking nature's beauty, and still ending up on my behind.

Yet when I do make it all the way down, I feel as if I am in better touch with nature, and in more than just the physical sense that it covers my entire lower body. I feel the lung-chilling clarity of listening to sounds being made on the spot. Of not having a medium between me and the outdoors. I change in my car, rinse my clothes out in the snow-cold river, and get ready for my fishing date.

At five o'clock, I meet Matt. If asked to describe him a week ago, I would have said he—big, bearded, small eyed—looked like a bear. Now that I am well versed in grizzly warnings, however, that's inaccurate. He is redder and paler. More Irish and much softer. His weight is well distributed on his six-foot-plus frame. He's around thirty, his hair and beard are a good red, and his hands are model worthy. He makes a quick effort to clean up his pickup before I get in, throwing empty soda bottles in the cab and clearing tapes off the passenger seat, apologizing for the mess. After so many hours in my own, it's weird being in another car, sitting next to a stranger, the window on my right instead of the left.

We drive south out of Livingston for a good twenty minutes before crossing a river and turning off on a dirt road. The sun is already pressing toward the horizon when we pull over behind another pickup where three guys gather, putting on their waders. Matt greets them and passes out introductions. Clicking on their suspenders and donning their lucky hats, they speak to one another of risers and floaters, seams and parachutes. Their waders, plastic and chest-high, look like large, dull clown pants. They are speaking gibberish. They're fabulous dorks. I feel comfortable immediately.

After the guys have taken off and Matt has outfitted himself, he leads me to the river. Having quizzed me on the details of my trip, Matt indulges me with details about where *A River Runs Through It* was shot.

"Do you remember the part in the movie where they take the girl's brother fishing?" Matt asks. "The city boy with the can of worms? That was filmed right here."

"Did the movie get a lot more city folk to come up here?"

"Yeah, I guess it got pretty crowded that summer, but ya know, it's always great seeing new folks enjoying the sport."

As we walk along the shore, the dimming light is already making the close trees look ashy. The river is shallow and sparkly and up ahead, I can see the guys' pale figures move against the mountains' dark mass. The white noise of insects and the hush of the river make it seem only quieter.

"All right," Matt says, kneeling a bit, "jump on."

"I'm sorry, what?"

"You want to get over the river, right? I've only got one pair of waders, so I gotta piggyback you across."

I do the demure girl thing. I don't mean to, but I haven't been piggybacked in more than twenty years, and the prospect makes me giddy.

"Don't worry, I've done this before. Haven't dropped one yet."

My first go, I'm giggling too much to get a good grip and slide off his back. I try again, locking my thighs around his hips, my fingers pressing into his shoulders. I realize I should probably wrap my arm around his neck, but somehow—despite the fact that my crotch is pressed into his back and his hands hold me hard under my legs—that seems too intimate.

The riverbed is a maze of mossy rocks, and Matt carefully plods over them. We have to do this twice to get to our intended island. Each time I feel the shift of weight from one foot to another and watch my knuckles pale from the pressure of digging into his shoulders. But if I'm weird and too tense, Matt acts as if I'm not. His back feels relaxed, secure. This river is his home, and after a while, his comfort is contagious.

Arriving at our hole, Matt stares down the river. "See that, those bubbles? In that hole? There's a riser. He's just waiting for us. Let's go over there and practice some casts."

His examples are a snap of the wrist and a rhythmic note in the air. They fall on the water's surface with the minimalism of a Picasso doodle. I follow his instructions. One to four o'clock, flick the wrist. My line flops ridiculously, the fly bundled up in line à la Jackson Pollock. Only a very stupid fish would bite at that. Still, Matt says kind things, such as I'm really good for a beginner and that I have a knack, and though I'm sure he is indulging me, I let myself believe him a little just the same.

After about ten minutes of practice casts and many compliments,

Matt tells me I'm ready for the hole. If only his encouraging words worked so well on the trout. Matt keeps up his pep talk, I think as much for the fish as for me.

"Here we go. Perfect. Right over 'im. He's gotta bite that." He also has a habit of saying, "There it is: Downtown Fishy Town." I forgive him that.

Matt went fishing 311 days last year. He *always* catches fish. He also *always* releases, unless he is backcountry and needs the food. He goes hunting now and again, mostly for elk, which are overpopulated and undernourished. He's had his eye on one buck for several weeks now and is looking forward to open season to give it a go. He'd like to make himself a deer tunic. I'm not so sure about that one—aesthetically, not ethically—but I forgive him that too.

Even though we will be out here for only about an hour, Matt brought one pole because I don't have a fishing license. As we take turns with the rod, he tells me about rules, written and not. Don't crowd other fishermen. His cast is a pluck of an acoustic string, the reeling in like pulling on a clean, quivering note. For a big guy, he has a gentle touch. Be quiet on the river, his voice purrs. Share the river. Listen to it. He talks to me about the fishing as if this is actually something I plan on pursuing, as if it's almost an insult to my talent if I do not.

"So do newcomers know about these rules?" I ask as if I no longer am one.

"Sometimes you'll get some city guy who sees you pull one in and will come stand right next to you like it's some kind of buffet. They can be . . . but no, no, I shouldn't say that. They are just beginners. They don't know better."

I keep baiting Matt to knock us urban folk but, like our fish, he never bites. It makes me think it's possible that biker wasn't just being nice. Stars are beginning to show themselves and twilight turns the river into black. The trees on the other side look murky. They aren't menacing; their edges just look less defined.

"Man, I'm sorry this fish is so spooked," Matt says with a sigh. "I really wanted you to catch something."

We walk and piggyback our way back to the pickup. As we drive back to Livingston, the conversation turns from fish to music to land to girls. He tells me about his ex-girlfriend as if he's never said it out loud. Out the window, Montana slips by. He invites me to come back to Yellowstone and he will take me backcountry. He invites me snowboarding. He invites me to crash at his place.

We get groceries and rent movies. He makes fajitas and we watch British flicks, me on the couch, him on the floor. His couch is the color of mustard and his walls are stark.

Matt touches me a couple of times. The back of his hand to my leg. Two fingers on my arm. He tells me some story, puts his hand on my knee and keeps it there.

I want to want Matt to slide his hand up my thigh. To lean in and kiss me in a way I don't think he can. To kiss him back. And if this were a script, I would. I would want it with all the emotion of a tense, string-heavy soundtrack. With the burn of a long, on-the-hunt buildup.

But this isn't, and though I really like Matt, the sex appeal he had on the river now escapes him. His efforts feel shy and forced, and though I want to want him, I don't. At all. I don't want him to touch me and I don't want to feel that I should. What's worse, I don't have the heart to tell him so. His hand still on my knee, I say I'm tired and turn into the couch. He tucks my covers up and mutters good night. I feign sleep, listening as he walks the distance to his room.

TEN SLEEP, WYOMING

In the morning, I try to stretch the sofa out of my spine and change in Matt's bathroom. Speaking through the door, Matt suggests we get coffee before I head off. Outside, September's first leaves litter the sidewalk. The wind is having its way with a few weak clouds. Everything else is still. We take separate vehicles into town, and Matt leads me to a café. It's painted waiting-room white and is decorated with half a dozen clocks, all counting down the time. At the counter, two teenage girls move in small circles—register to coffee to plastic lids—and in the front of the shop, several middle-aged men gather around a low table.

The men are noticeable. Their faces hold hard angles and they talk heatedly. While I wait in line, Matt joins them. From the counter, I watch his features turn different from any way I've seen them before. His jaw flexes. His brow tightens. He looks at me, holding the expression, and I smile back, unsuccessfully trying to soften it. He turns back to the men. It's then that I concentrate on what they are saying. It's something about planes. About New York. Matt approaches and looks at me dead-on, his voice steadier than his expression. He tells me that planes have flown into the World Trade Center. The whole of Montana's sky is suddenly impossibly heavy. The weight of it forces my mouth open and my throat closed. Tears surprise me.

I look blankly back at Matt. "I don't get TV reception," he says. "Let's go to Brian's."

Matt speeds down the streets and rolls fast through stop signs. I follow him in my car, listening to the radio as I go. The voices are breathy and disbelieving. Facts are vague. I briefly lose Matt around a curve before I see him stopped in front of a small house. He gets out, unlatches a short gate where a wire-haired dog bounces obliviously, and walks into the house. I follow several steps behind.

"Wake up, man. You're not gonna believe this."

Brian joins us on the couch. We sit, watching it over and over and over again, feeding on the repetition, hanging on each Unconfirmed. Time runs in a looping, commercial-free standstill. Someone on the TV says it's like a movie, but *Die Hard* never made me feel like this. We make comments. The guys make phone calls. They repeat the phrases we said to each other into the phone and repeat to us the phrases they heard back, all of us looking for words that fit.

Matt should go to work, I to Wyoming. We watch still. We talk about who did it and war and the draft and *My god, the bodies*, and hush when the TV shows a new angle or witness. We listen to the screams and watch the distant deaths. To make it less real. Or maybe to make it more.

Eventually, after many hours that, absent of the network's normal markings of time, seem so much more, the information hits a plateau and I step back. The images are an addiction and right now, I feel I've got to get out. I hug Matt goodbye. It feels oddly hollow, as if we're pressing together inanimate versions of ourselves.

Back in my car, I point my car south, listening again to the news. The land flattens and grays. Mountains make up the horizon. A river drags to my right. The radio reception sputters, and when it goes to white noise, I listen to it still. The static somehow sounds good.

Static carries me into Wyoming. To Yellowstone. The entrance is unspectacular, but a couple of cars stop for a photo op just the same, their destination now reached. Inside the park, the scenic pullouts are full of awkward crowds. They wear weird smiles for the cameras, trying to go on with their family vacations.

"So, where are you from? Oh, yeah, we flew in from Long Beach last week. . . . We don't know how we're getting home." Grimace. "I don't . . . I mean . . . it's just horrible." I understand, but it's too much. I can't talk about it. I can't talk about anything else. There are too many variations in land and people and circumstance, and all talk feels small, even though it's not.

In this space where everything is foreign, my car is my steady. I keep driving through the park. Every thirty minutes there is a new alien landscape. A rough grass field quickly gives way to a pine forest to a red dirt bluff to a sulfur moonscape back to a flowered prairie. The changes are fast and vast; I get my bearings in a scene only when a new one forces itself upon it. Occasionally I stop out of obligation. I watch one buffalo mount another. He kicks up a cloud of dust. I walk around the bubbling sulfur springs. I see a river otter slide around a waterfall's off-flow. And, where a fire scarred the forest, I stop and sit. Acre after acre of hillside is studded with the silhouettes of thorny trunks. From a distance, they're millions of simple black brushstrokes on a canvas. Up close, they're skinny and charred, standing defiantly from the ground but tapering to a withered, limb-less point. The traffic of the park's more scenic routes gone, I sit alone at the pullout, staring out. The austerity would be too much if it weren't for the green sprouting under the dead trunks. As is, I could sit here for hours. The landscape's numbing melancholy gives space to my own.

I carry on past Yellowstone Lake, through the Shoshone For-est, and out of the park. The trees segue into soil. Driving east on a thin road, surrounded by cliffs the color of ocher, I listen to the radio, whose reception has returned. News is perpetual, yet information is scarce. Testimonials are endless. I pull through Cody, a wide-necked town of loud signs and cowboy kitsch, and though the day is darkening, this place is not right, not tonight. I continue, taking smaller roads through Bighorn Basin, where the land is long and tanned.

A little while later, I'm brought into a short canyon. The rusted bluffs are flat topped and streaked with minerals and it's the time of day when the sky can do no wrong: all warm and amber and riding-into-the-sunset red. I stop for gas in a six-shop town called Ten Sleep. Across from the Arco is a small wood-cabin motel and next to that, a white chapel. It has a sign out: PRAYER FOR THE VICTIMS OF WTC. 7 PM.

In the motel, I turn on the TV before putting down my bags, and then I shower and get dressed listening to the news. Already it looks different. Those loose falling bodies, the gruesome unedited moments of honesty, have been tucked away somewhere safe. Upper-right screen graphics have been made and slogans set. Mayor Giuliani of New York is speaking at a conference. He is gaunt and wears devastation on every crease in his face. Perched on the end of the bed watching him, my chest hurts as if I know him.

I make phone calls to friends and talk to my mom, who, for the first time, is actually relieved I'm on this trip: I couldn't be much farther from a terrorist target. Then I go into the chapel. The room's white and square. It looks like a classroom but for the flower wreath of dyed blue carnations and baby's breath at the altar. The pastor whispers to me that it's a silent prayer. Thank God. I sit in the back on the side, my head down. When I get restless, I steal looks at the other eight people sitting around the room. All of us drawn here. For its sense of community. For its respite from the news. Because we feel helpless, and more than anywhere else, here, this feels okay.

CHAPTER FOUR

Close Encounters of the Third Kind

(Contemplating the lump shape)
"This means something. This is important."

[ROY, CLOSE ENCOUNTERS OF THE THIRD KIND]

I 've never had much loyalty to formal institutions. I'm wary of the iconography their symbols take on. The few times I've attended religious ceremonies with friends, I've watched with the same perspective I have when watching a nature program: appreciative, but without much personal application. This is also true for the institution of America.

I grew up under the umbrella of Berkeley, where America was something less to identify with than to rally against. When abroad, I've usually been the first to critique American culture as commercial, superficial, and self-absorbed. I knew no other country was less flawed, that I was lucky to be able to express the disagreements I had, and furthermore, that I too was commercial, superficial, and self-absorbed, but this still never instilled much pride.

When I wake, none of this has necessarily changed. It was a fitful night in Ten Sleep. I fell asleep to the public bereavement on the network news, never finding a moment when it felt okay to turn it off. In the morning, the anchormen's suits look the same but their faces seem indeterminably older. The night wore down the horror, leaving a more naked sadness, and I want out of the motel room and into the womb of my car.

Yes, if asked, I'd still say America can be a bully. But now, suffering a blow to its gut, bent over and windless, it also seems so much more. I drive east out of Ten Sleep, through more tiger-striped canyons, over the Bighorn Mountains, and into the choppy prairie land of Devils Tower.

■ ■ ■ ■ ■ ■ ■ ■ ■

Thirty dull miles from any town of note, Devils Tower, the giant stump of rock that juts out of Wyoming's northeast corner, is not a place one just happens upon; it must be sought out. And many do. For centuries, the Arapaho, Crow, Lakota, Cheyenne, Kiowa, and Shoshone tribes have journeyed to its base, using it as a sacred site for prayer offerings, sweat lodge ceremonies, and vision quests. Naturalists gravitate to its unique ecosystem, geologists go to study the tower's sixty-million-year-old magma, and climbers pull themselves up the Tower's crevices for a notch in their thick-harnessed belts. Almost five thousand people a year scale the Tower's 857 feet. Retirees migrate to the landmark—its nearby KOA was once voted the best campground between Yellowstone and Chicago—and hogs are big there, too.

The Tower is an official stop in Sturgis's annual Black Hills Rally, and as many as two hundred thousand bikers congregate at its base in early August, when the world's largest Harley-Davidson flag flies. Devils Tower also worked its magic on one Steven Spielberg, who used it as the alien mecca in his 1979 film, *Close Encounters of the Third Kind.* More than twenty years after its release, fans of the film still replicate Richard Dreyfuss's pilgrimage to the Tower.

Now I count myself among those who come here for a purpose, even if I'm at a loss to explain what exactly it is. For the last twenty-four hours, in the middle of near nowhere, I've felt spun loose. The vague goals I came here with—to see how Wyoming compared to my expectations, to see if *Close Encounters* had any lingering effects on my unconscious—seem senseless and trite

But this morning, I don't know; I find myself with more in

common with that movie than I'd ever expected. I feel inexplicably drawn to the Tower. I was only six or seven at the time I first saw it. It was the first movie I ever saw on home video. I remember then being curious about Devils Tower. Dreyfuss's obsession was contagious. All those people flocking to the rock made me want to see it myself. But now, it feels like more than just curiosity—it feels like need. For all my other abstracted hopes of self-discovery, I originally left home because I wanted to get to know this country better. And for some reason, right now this odd lump of rock seems to offer a way to.

As I near the rock, my eyes scan the horizon. I thought that the area around the Tower would be paper flat, and that the rock would punctuate the slate like a fat, flat-topped phallus. I kinda thought I'd be able to see its signature stub from across the state. Instead, the land is bumpy and butted, and though when I do see it, its shape is instantly recognizable, its size is hardly jaw-dropping. When I pull closer and am forced to look up at the Tower, yes, it's mighty and tall, but it also looks like an oversized thimble.

It's pretty scratched up, too. Resting on a rise of trees and chunky rocks, the Tower is grooved into hundreds of columns, not unlike the fork-striated mashed potatoes in *Close Encounters*. The geological explanation is that molten magma rose underground and, when cooling, it contracted and fractured, the erosion of the softer surrounding landscape later revealing its form. I prefer the local Plains tribes' version.

Though we know it as Devils Tower, the Native American name for the rock is Mateo Tepee, or Bear's Lodge. They say seven sisters running from a grizzly jumped on a low rock and prayed to it to help them. The rock obediently pushed itself upward, and as the bear reached after them, it scratched its claws down the rock's sides. The girls were safe, but the rock is the worse for wear.

I enter the park and rest my car in a parking lot that resembles a small, boxy town, the few parking spots not claimed by RVs poised like driveways to their doors. The sitting areas are populated by an older set, some genial and as mobile as their homes, others who crouch like sitcom gags, complaining about the park fee and the walk from the car. A few others like me lower the median age. Climbers wearing rope sashes like pageant contestants and gravity-defying confidence beeline to the Tower, aware of nothing but the Rock. Walking to the visitors center, I pass park workers standing all smiles. Several young parents tend to small running whining things. It's been only a day, but already the family photo ops seem less guilty, their laughter less inappropriate.

At the park center, geological pictograms illustrate the Tower's gradual exposure, showing it as it looked in the days of dinosaurs and early man. I look at the black and white photographs that tell the Tower's more recent history, when this area still had bears and buffalo and Plains tribes. Here, my strange draw to the Tower actually seems to make sense. So much of the Tower's story is a story of America and I cling to it.

Though the Tower has been revealing itself for millions of years, modern documentation dates it to the arrival of white people. Back then, the Tower and its surroundings didn't promise much, and the new American government, trying to ease its entry into more profitable areas, signed a pact promising it to the local Plains tribes. Alas, it wasn't six years before it took the Tower back. Gold was found in the Black Hills, Custer fought the Battle of Little Bighorn to clear the area for whites, ranchers moved in, and Mateo Tepee quickly changed from a sacred native site to Devils Tower, a place for the new residents to hold Fourth of July cookouts. Some of these ranchers had bigger ideas for the Tower. One petitioned the government to build an iron stairway to the summit. Others wanted to make it a resort. But in 1906, on the heels of the national parks' success, Roosevelt staved off development by inducting Devils Tower as America's first national monument.

The monument today has two paths around it: an asphalt trail that circles its perimeter and a longer dirt one that takes a more wayward route through the landscape. I start off with the short trail, but even though it's not that busy, the other tourists seem to crowd me. They walk in small groups and make innocuous comments. They make me inexplicably uncomfortable. It's particular, too, this strangeness. It's not like in Washington, or even in Montana, where my issues seemed rooted in loneliness. I no longer feel that sharp center of self-pity. I'm tempted to say it's because now such feelings are petty, or because some of my anti-Americanism collapsed along with those towers, that my discomfort is the result of grief, or even of identifying with people I hereto held as different. And yet, though parts of those reasons may be true, I fear it's not the real source of my unease. I turn around. The head of the longer trail leads into the trees and I enter it.

The land here is dry and tweedy; the ground looks like a Boy Scout's badge material. The only bit of color comes from the ribbons tied to a few of the trees' lower branches; nearby signs explain them as offerings left by Native Americans and ask that visitors leave them undisturbed. The trail is refreshingly empty, and, as in Yellowstone, the land it covers is well spliced for those with stunted attention spans. One moment I'm listening to the woods' continual call-and-response, the snaps of branches, and the high pitch of birds, and the next I'm on a dry knoll with only wind and low brush for company. A few more minutes along, the dirt is so red and fine, it tints my socks and congeals my spit into a thick red paint. This cedes to a low plain goose-bumped with prairie dogs' mounded front doors.

But no matter how grand the scenery, all of it pales next to that rock. It stands there like a massive tree stump, like a boss over my shoulder. Sometimes its shape changes. From some angles, it seems to slouch like the retirees in its lot. Walk a little longer, though, and it straightens into something browner and slimmer: the climbers and the Kiowa. Even its lines look less creased, until another change of light and position, and its spine again loses its symmetry and its red walls turn back to ash. No matter its shape, though, it is always there. Even with my back turned, taking in a view, I can feel it big above me. It intimidates me when I dare look elsewhere. It dares me to take it on.

It also makes me wonder how the hell Dreyfuss got on top of that thing. Back at the visitors station, I read about the Tower's first climber: a local rancher who, in 1893, spent a month building a foot ladder out of wooden pegs to the summit, a ladder that has long since disintegrated. From where I stand now, I can see several climbers near the top, their color like faraway fireworks on a gray sky. I mean, I think I recall a few scenes of Dreyfuss's scrambling up some rocks. I think he had some rope, but I certainly don't remember his suiting up in gear good for climbing a sheer face.

Dreyfuss's immaculate ascent wouldn't normally bug me. I'd figure there was some scrappy route and never give it a second thought. But I'm here, though, and the rock taunts me. The climbers' voices carry easily, and I can almost make out what they say. They make me jealous, the climbers. And not for the reasons they usually do—their ability to pull their own weight and look impressive in a tank top—or even for the reasons I've envied other groups on this trip: for their comradeship. I'm still preferring being out here alone.

No, right now I just want to be on top of that thing.

Maybe it's just human nature. Something that big hangs over you and dwarfs you; you either want to own it or serve it. You want it to make sense. The Tower rises from Earth like an offering, otherworldly and weird. Again, I'm not a big believer in higher powers, but staring at the rock, I almost want to be. It seems a shame if a higher being—god or green man—didn't exist, so perfectly suited it is for their worship.

But I can't climb it. And I don't really pray. So instead, I circle and circle, looking up at it whenever I can. From my spot near the trail's end, I can see how the erosion of rainwater and the Wyoming wind have smoothed its crown. Its top slopes like the tip of a thumb. Staring at it fills me with wonder. If only for the moment I'm looking up at it, it makes me feel less lost.

■ ■ ■ ■ ■ ■ ■ ■ ■ ■

Parked next to the row of Harleys outside the Devils Tower Trading Post, my car looks like a cartoon. I've left the park and come here because, in my experience, as nice as the official national park gift shops are— refined and educational and so well thought out—for the true consumer experience, the shops outside the official borders are the better bet. Leaving my car to fend for itself, I find this one is no exception. The magnets alone would dwarf the stock of most Third World grocery stores. Commemorative spoons and Devils Tower paperweights.

Decorative plates and snowballs. It even smells like America. A food counter in the back sells corn dogs and cheese fries. I imagine the fryer oil in the air gives my hair a nice sheen.

Back in Oakland, I had these neighbors who were part Cherokee. They liked to tend to their front garden and talk politics, and on Sundays, when my roommates and I shared the paper on the front porch, we often discussed the headlines. Anyway, I remember this one day—I think school prayer was making its rounds through the courts—when they told us about this sacred rock popular with climbers. They said a coalition of Native tribes had tried to get an injunction against climbing the rock for the month of June. In their eyes, climbers on their rock were akin to people's driving stakes in the Grace Cathedral, and they wanted just one month so they could perform ceremonies without the distraction the climbers presented.

At the time, I never connected their rock to the Tower I saw in a Spielberg movie. And I probably never would've, except that, in my craving to climb it myself, I've picked up one of the store's climbing company's pamphlets and noticed it offers no tours in June. I remember the rest of their story: The park service supported the one-month ban, but it could only make it voluntary. Devils Tower is under federal authority, and because the U.S. government deems Native traditions exercises of "land-based religion," a court ruled a climbing prohibition would be giving religion precedence over the Tower's other uses. In a strange twist that confused who's state and what's church, the June ban was seen as a violation of the Constitution's separation between them.

It also reminds me of a story I read at the visitors' center about that first rancher to climb the Tower. He made his ascent on the Fourth of July to a crowd of thousands. When he reached the top, he unfurled the American flag, which the wind promptly—some would say poetically—blew off. His promoters tore it up and sold it as souvenirs.

I put back the brochure—who am I kidding? I can't even do a pull-up—and wander the gift shop. Still preferring solitude, I stay clear of the Trading Post's other patrons. I check out the Harley bullet-hole stickers—you, too, can have that drive-by look!—and the shirts of eagles wearing flag bandannas and posters of half-clad biker babes, the red, white, and blue just visible on the straps of their thongs. Really, I have no problem with the "Under God" in our pledge, or with politicians' current calls for prayer. And while I think it noble that we try to partition church and state, it's always seemed to me as ambitious as a preteen pledging abstinence: Easy in theory. Hard in practice. Religion is so tied up in tradition and ritual, belonging and community, patriotism and economy that sometimes it's impossible to separate it from culture and culture from it. I mean, even this gift shop feels a little congregational. The Native American rosaries are represented in dream catchers and sage bundles, the climbers' in clamp-ons and victory shirts, and for the cinephile, there are scrawny green men postcards and by the cash register, a pile of original, twenty-year-old packages of *Close Encounters* gum and playing cards.

Like other movies I saw when I was young, *Close Encounters* is no more to me now than a handful of images. The mashed potatoes. The music. Oddly, I also remember the scene in which people lined the freeway to the Tower, holding signs and hawking goods. Even at my young age, it must have struck me as true: that such a phenomenon would inspire both prophets—soothsayers decrying the end of the world—and profits—T-shirts, pins, and apocalyptic souvenirs.

And I wonder why I'm so uneasy in company; were I offered conversation, I couldn't trust what I would say. It's been only a day, but my cynicism has already settled back in, and unlike cynicism's normally nice, righteous glow, right now it's making me feel pretty damn bad. The flag shirts on sale for a special discount make me sad, yet under that confusedly mad, too. As awful as I feel for succumbing to my skepticism so soon, I hear the woman at the counter tell a customer, "God bless America," and I have to fight back a cringe.

But if I'm a dubious patriot and a bad American, I'm not where it counts. At the register, I pull out my wallet. I buy a Devils Tower magnet and a sticker for my car. I know this country is so much more. Too bad it's so much easier to pick a point of view and call it a day. Next to the cash register is a postcard of Devils Tower looking grand and iconic and just as it should. I add it to the pile.

In the car, I pull out my map and turn on the radio. The Christian station is the only one with decent reception and I listen, interested in what it has to say today. The attacks are a message from God. Repent. We are in a holy war. I talk back to the radio, annoyed that the speakers take such liberties with their analogies. These towers weren't a symbol of God, you assholes. They didn't bomb our churches. They hit our Trade Center.

But these are blasphemous thoughts right now. It's too early. I'm too cruel. I turn off the radio, rally some hurt in me, and find my place on my United States road atlas. I've never been so surrounded by America: to the north and south, right and left. Nor have I ever felt both such a part of a larger thing and yet so alien to it. The Midwest sits on my map with all the expression of an unfurrowed forehead. I plunge in.

DEADWOOD, SOUTH DAKOTA

Leaving Wyoming, I drive east to the Black Hills of South Dakota. I never imagined the state had so many trees. I wind around the curves and into the casinos of Deadwood. It's the only hostel listing I have from Seattle to Minneapolis.

Alas, when I finally get there, I find the hostel is actually a studio-size motel room with three bunk beds. I have to angle myself sideways to get to the bathroom. I can wash my hands without getting out of bed. A TV is attached to the ceiling, as in hospital rooms, and since I have a penchant for top bunks and the ceilings are low, the TV is just inches above my feet.

Even before Tuesday's attacks, my time with television on this trip has been excessive. Back home, I watched maybe five hours a week. On the road, I've been averaging that a night. Returning from a beer in strange bar, with no witnesses to call me on my gluttony, it has felt awfully good to turn on that familiar chatter and forget myself. Some-

how, the television has given me distance from my circum-
stances while curiously connecting me at the same time; as
if I haven't been alone in these motel rooms when a million
others were watching *ER,* too. It isn't until morning when
I feel the effect. I wake with a dieter's resolve: *Today I'll be
good. I'll stay out longer. I won't even turn it on once.*

Yet here I am again, in another blank room. I've already
gone into town, eaten, and lingered. Over my shell shock,
I crave conversation, anyone to help make the images less
abstract, but no one is around; everyone is home watching the news from New York. Back in my room, I fight my
temptation to do the same.

I listen to the low groan of the few passing cars.
Silence. Minutes pass, then distant footsteps. I hear a metallic *clunk* as the drink machine drops a soda, followed with
the high-pitched tinkle of change. Footsteps back. A door
creaks and closes. Silence again. Nothing.

Yet all it takes is a switch. And boom: dust, talk,
names, lines, scars, tears. Men and steel. The sad hope for
one breathing body. No, it's not like a movie, not at all. Days
have passed, the images are now more familiar, the stories
packaged into a format I've seen before. Still, it's far more
real than anything else I've seen on-screen.

More real, even, than this blank room I'm in.

This is new. I mean, I've experienced media events before, but never anything like this. Gazing at the scenes in New York feels like a duty, like participation, like mourning, even. I think, *This can't be right. This can't be the way an experience is measured.* But right now, it's the only way I know how.

I'm wondering what it will feel like to be in New York in several weeks' time, how different from these pictures it will be, when, outside, a car pulls up. Two female voices emerge, move toward the office. Several minutes later, they jangle by the car again, and then at my room's door. I turn off the volume as the girls come in, bent under their backpacks. They throw down their weight, say hellos. They're on a three-week road trip and have been camping in their Volkswagen. It's good to be in a room. One of them looks up to the TV as an afterthought.

"Any new info?"

"Not much," I realize. "No."

They lay a map down on the several square feet of empty floor and sit around it: "Well, we could go over to Rushmore and then hang north to Yellowstone. . . ."

The news is still on. They don't want to watch. Maybe

I'm just jealous, but they don't seem to care. I can criticize the nature of my participation, but I can't imagine not being beholden to it. I turn off the mute and watch some more.

CHAPTER FIVE

Fargo

"And I guess that was your
accomplice in the wood chipper."

[MARGE, FARGO]

North Dakota is the least visited of all the fifty states.

I once saw a segment—I think it was an early incarnation of MADtv—investigating why. Some poor soul was reporting from a wide, comically white space. She looked like Kenny from *South Park*. All you could see was a cinched hood of fur, and she stood by a statue of Lawrence Welk—renowned accordion player and North Dakota native—muffling observations on the fact that it was, well, cold.

North Dakota is a punch line.

After Bart got *The Simpsons* expelled from Australia, they were shown a United States map of all the states from which they were banned. Only North Dakota was exempt. An *X Files* episode brought Mulder and Scully to North Dakota because someone wanted to hide a UFO where no one would find it. The state was also used in a bit on *The West Wing*, based on an actual North Dakotan proposal to drop the "North" from its name:

> **North Dakota Representative:** *Are you aware that studies clearly show the word "North" leaves the impression that this state is cold, snowy, and flat, significantly depressing tourism and business start-up?*
>
> **White House Rep:** *With due respect, sir, your average temperature is seven degrees, your average snowfall, forty-two inches, and a name change isn't going to take care of that.*
>
> **North Dakota Rep:** *We enjoy roughly the same climate as South Dakota. We took in 73.7 million in tourism revenue last year. They took in 1.2 billion. They have the word "South."*
>
> **White House Rep:** *Also Mount Rushmore.*

Then there's the Coen brothers' *Fargo*. A fun story of kidnapping, murder, and gory, disfiguring mishap, *Fargo* relied as much on North Dakota as it did on the comedic talents of William H. Macy and Frances McDormand. The area's unique language and landscape set much of the movie's droll tone.

This running mockery of North Dakota would probably slide by me, subtle assumptions of a cold, sorry-ass state aside, if it weren't for the fact that Sarah, my housemate back in Oakland, is from there. She grew up in the small towns of Bison and Rugby, and just as knowing someone with a mental illness makes you sensitive to the word "crazy," so has knowing Sarah made me aware of every potshot thrown her home state's way.

Having a North Dakotan as a housemate also means I feel I've gotten to know the place a little already. Back in Oakland, we received copies of the small-town paper her sister worked for. Every article and picture carried her byline. The paper's headlines were always entertaining, its crime log so cute. And when her sister visited Oakland, she would amuse us with tales straight out of Lake Wobegon. How the alcohol the cops confiscated from minors was saved for the annual Fireman's Ball. The two cops: one morbidly obese, who couldn't walk a block without stopping to sit, the other, who'd recently had a stroke and suffered from short-term memory loss, perpetually locking his keys in the station and squad car.

For the last five years, we've also always had a North Dakota calendar in our kitchen. "See, isn't it beautiful?" Sarah would say and I'd nod, aware that the last five calendars had shared the same twelve shots. "North Dakota may not have South Dakota's tourist draws, but it has far more class," she'd continue, sounding like a sibling bitter over her sister's popularity. That argument usually struck me as sort of sad—it's easy

to claim you're above selling out when no one wants what you're selling—but on this, I'd indulge her. What else had North Dakotans got?

I'm surprised, then, driving up out of the Black Hills and along the
Etch-a-Sketch lines that are North Dakotan roads, to find the state sorta
pretty. True, it's flat and without a lot of fancy colors. There are few
curves, and passing the random car doesn't rouse the slightest adrenaline, but the road has slow rolls that lull my mind. I'm especially surprised because I've been dreading this day's drive since the day I left
for this trip. Looking at the map of the long bland land through North
Dakota to Sarah's parents' house, I imagined the state working like an
isolation chamber, its vacuum forcing my brain to feed on itself, seduc-
ing me into delusions, mirages, and imaginary friends. Instead, I find
the absence of stimuli welcome. After the past few days fixed on TV's
busy designs and multiplying story angles, the prairie sweeps me clean.

I drive on. Open. Empty. My car keeps a straight course while my
brain follows twisted trails—thoughts of fifth-grade fashion turn to
questions of global politics to consideration of death and remembrances
of sex. I think and yet register none of it. I concentrate on my posture at
times, tightening my muscles around their dull sitting aches. Pay attention to my music's lyrics. Talk into the tape recorder about the state's
National Grassland and the fact that, as nice as it is, it's hard to muster
much enthusiasm for a field of grass. I talk about the sky's flatness. The
sky in Montana felt big because it was so deep. Punctuated by granite

masses and reaching down rivers' walls, the sky was thick and filled the air like flesh. Here, like pictures drawn in grade school, land and sky meet in a thin-lipped line. The sky is absolutely all over—I can't look anywhere it's not—yet it feels as light as tissue, as if I could poke through it with a finger.

The more I drive, the more North Dakota grows on me. It has the beauty of someone who isn't trying and is more stunning because of it. I notice the heaviness in my shoulders. Twist my neck. Clench my butt. Think about muscle atrophy and Latin word roots and Egypt's pyramids and the jacket in *Desperately Seeking Susan. Is this what freedom feels like,* I wonder, *or is it boredom?*

■ ■ ■ ■ ■ ■ ■ ■ ■ ■

Sarah's parents live in Tioga, a small town off a farm road in central North Dakota. Her mom is affectionate, jovial, a proud, Nordic-descent North Dakotan. Her father's a Lutheran pastor, contemplative, Canadian. They take me into town for their friend Laura Jean's birthday and introduce me to their friends. I play with their spaniel, whose name I always thought was "Bomber" until Sarah's dad tells me his girls made him change its spelling according to his pacifist teachings. "It's 'Balmer' now," he says. I discover the source of my roommate's love of pickles, Nordic designs, and well-folded linen. I rediscover the comfort of someone else taking care of me.

Sitting at their kitchen table over good coffee, Sarah's father asks how I've taken the last week. He has a way of centering his attention on you that makes you feel you matter. He's read about the death of irony, about how this will change my generation. He wonders how I feel. I'm not sure what exactly irony is about. Cleverness? Emotional distance? he offers. Her mom pours refills. I say I've never been afraid of my emotions, just of what triggers them. Is there a difference? he asks. I think so. I thought so. There has to be. Between artifice and sincerity. Between reacting to the expectations they each set. He nods as I go on. I talk about the news, as if it's an explanation. How I distrust it. How I need it. How I'm not sure what scares me more, my numbness to it, or the ways it gets me still. I try to talk my way through it. I talk too much.

My time in Tioga is wonderful. I could melt at that kitchen table, given enough time. The road, though, is working its rhythm on me. As warm as their hospitality is, after a month on my own it's awkward playing guest. By the third morning, I actually miss my car. I repack my car and hug goodbyes. I leave for Fargo thinking that I quite like the Midwest.

■■■■■■■■■

A true story. In November 2001, two months from now, a young Japanese woman named Takako Konoshi will be found wandering a road outside of Bismarck, North Dakota, clutching a crude map of a road drawn on a white sheet of paper. She'll speak no English and the cops will do their best body language, but to no avail. They'll even contact all the Chinese restaurants in town. No one in town speaks Japanese. She'll keep pointing at her map, offering an explanation they can't understand, and they'll repeat back to her the only word they do. "Fargo?" they'll ask. "Fargo," she'll answer with a grin. One of the cops will look at the map again and come up with an answer: She's here because of the movie, looking for the loot the kidnappers buried by the roadside.

He will try to tell her it's not real, that though the Coens introduced the movie by claiming it was a true story, they actually made it up. It's no use. They can't get through. And though they doubt her sanity, seeing as she's not breaking any laws and they don't know what else to do with her, they'll help her continue her journey, seeing her on a bus to Fargo.

It's a very *Fargo* story. And it would be a funny one but for the ending. Several days later, she'll be found by a Minnesotan lake, dead from overdose and exposure.

I take a road that cuts across to Fargo. It is obscenely straight and, compared to the drive north from Deadwood, equally dull. The sky is bland, and between the road kill that decorates the shoulders, the insect population thickening on my windshield, and the slow towns I speed by—many of which Sarah's dad told me are losing as much as 10 percent of their population a decade—I feel surrounded by carnage. Not that it's ugly, exactly, but the land is flat and straight and glum. I can only imagine how blinding it must be with snow.

I pull into Fargo around four o'clock. This . . . this is ugly.

Absolutely and fantastically unattractive. And I say this as someone who tends to like the ugly. Like many of my peers, I can find the glow of authenticity in the most grungy scenes, but I've got to hand it to Fargo for being really, really hideous. I enter the city via its auto row, where *Fargo* was filmed. Like its roads, the local architects seem unfamiliar with curves: Large buildings sit low and square, boasting all the charms of cardboard boxes. The light outside is cold, bright, harsh. The signs are uninspired, the decorative balloons depressing. The streets look littered even where they are not, and where the evenness of North Dakota's countryside was serenely empty, Fargo's flat skyline has the negative space of something missing. I feel as if I'm in a pit.

I remember when I first saw *Fargo* in college with one of my more sensitive friends. While I walked out laughing, she was horrified. She, too, believed the Coens when they said it was true and was galled they could make such fun of multiple murders. At the time, I mocked her for taking the movie so seriously, but now I drive, searching its truths. Is this what Sarah's father meant by irony? I pass the parking lots and deserted streets, looking for its downtown. Even when I'm out of auto row, the stores still look like it: the boxes advertising window tinting and stereo installation replaced with boxes for Used-A-Bit Sales and Grocery Outlets. The Big Top

Bingo Hall, a low, wide building the size of a city block labeled with a triangular picture of a circus roof. As big as the sign is, it can't compensate for the fact that it's a sign sitting on a box of no inherent wonder.

I eventually find the cluster of buildings barely three stories high that constitutes downtown. This architecture is more interesting, but there is no one around and nothing to do. I get directions to the motels off the freeway. The interstate beats movement—veins of red and white pulsing opposite directions—and on the streets, cars thump and honk and race to the next stoplight. Here, the boxes are Applebee's and Taco John and Kmart and Macy's. They shine newer, brighter signs and are surrounded by supersize lots, headlights buzzing around their neon like bugs. At an intersection where three of the four corners are claimed by gas stations, I find a Motel 6. I pay my $29.95 and go back downtown to find some food. The diner echoes; a chat with my college-aged waitress confirms my fears. I ask her where I should go out at night.

"Well, where are you staying?" she asks.

"At a Motel 6 off the freeway. Near a Burger King."

"Oh," she says enviously, "you're where all the action is!"

■■■■■■■■■■

The next afternoon, another waitress slides me a plate. "Soooo, that will duuuez yaaah?" Her voice lilts high and low like a slow-motion polka.

"Yep. Thanks," I respond, sounding as if I'm on speed. So far, my housemate's pledge that the *Fargo* accent was exaggerated seems true. I've heard "Ya betcha" only twice, and where some of the actors sounded like Swedes doing a Southern drawl, I've instead found a patient sing-song in people's speech that I quite like. I've been impressed with what some of the older locals can do with the word "ya" and how sentences linger as if in no great rush to finish themselves.

"Okeeah then," the waitress says and returns to her lean by the cash register. Today, I've come searching for Fargo at its downtown VFW. Somewhere in my subconscious, I know VFW stands for Veterans Something-or-Other, but when I first walk into the off-colored corner restaurant stamped with the letters, all I can think of is Vehement Flag Waving. I've seen a lot of flags on the road the last several days, but the VFW really went to town. There are red, white, and blue banners hung on the counters and walls and along the entranceway to the attached meeting hall. Flags wrap around the tables' Orangina bottles, and they drape from the windows and doorjambs and picture frames and the cash register. One can't even season one's home fries without a patriotic reminder: Each individual salt and pepper shaker is tied with a trio of colored ribbons.

At the counter, an obese man sits with a flyswatter, looking better suited to an Alabaman porch than to this North Dakotan diner. He wears a short-sleeve button-down shirt, only the second button of which is done, and he faces the window where I sit, affording me a prime view of his bare stomach. It's wide and pinkish and spills over the upper part of his pants. He compensates for the bulk of him that won't fit on the barstool by planting a foot on the floor, and he makes running commentary to the two waitresses and four other customers at the counter about the attacks on America. "I'll tell yaaah, we're gonna hunt 'em down. This aaall kaaayda, they're not gonna know what hit 'em." Occasionally, one nods, but most just sit listening, knowing nothing more is expected of them.

As the fat man continues, I dig into my eggs, sausage, and flapjacks. While the coffee in the last couple of states has been unilaterally piss-poor, the breakfasts have been unparalleled. I've taken to ordering them regardless of the hour. Outside, a police siren beeps briefly, and I pause to watch as a cop pulls over behind an early seventies brown sedan. The driver looks in his rearview mirror while the cop walks stiff legged to his window. Everyone at the counter is rapt. Well, maybe that word is too enthusiastic, but they all turn to watch and the waitresses come to check on my coffee, getting a better look.

"Hummph . . . now, I don't recognize that car," the fat man says. The siren's lights turn silently. "See, now, he's looking him up," he continues, fanning himself with his flyswatter. "You just never know. Not in this day and age."

I seriously doubt his insinuation that Bin Laden is sending operatives to North Dakota in late-model sedans, but after my day in Fargo, it's nice to hear something so presumptuous. I spent all morning circling the city's uninspired grid of blocks and lots. The depression was consistent.

Relentless. The only thing I found not slouched in self-contempt turned out not to even count. I happened upon it when I was lost. A snow-white, twin-masted fiberglass tent, the Hjemkomst Heritage Center rose from the city's blocks like an Ice Queen's Cirque du Soleil. Big Top Bingo had to be jealous. Inside, light shined through the opaque roof onto a massive seventy-six-foot-long Viking ship. Built by a local guidance counselor to sail back to his ancestral home of Norway, the *Hjemkomst*'s ivory sails stretched like the most ambitious slide projector screens. It was a grand vision in this flat space. Except it turned out this place wasn't Fargo. As the woman at the information desk took pains to point out, I was actually now in the neighboring Minnesotan city of Moorhead. I looked around at the center's Scandinavian souvenirs, at its proud information on Moorhead history and culture, even on how the area's oft-mocked dialect derives from Scandinavian speech patterns. And then I looked at the Fargo souvenirs. T-shirts that read: LONDON. ROME. PARIS. FARGO. Coffee mugs imprinted with YAH BETCHA like it's the city's slogan.

Back at the diner, still watching the driver and cop, I sort through brochures I picked up at the museum, searching them for anything else to do. Not that the standoff outside isn't thrilling, but Fargo has a population of ninety thousand, and I refuse to believe things are really so slow that this constitutes a good time. One of the brochures states the remarkable fact that in a recent survey compiled by the Fujifilm Corporation, Fargo was voted the least photogenic metropolitan area in the nation.

Think of that: In all America, Fargo was the ugliest. The abuse just doesn't stop.

I'm intrigued, then, that the Plains Art Museum brochure says it's showcasing an artist who was commissioned to work on Fargo's architecture. Or rather, it says, in the self-deprecating tone that I'm learning to associate with this town, that the young woman "has undertaken an unenviable task: She has set her sights on creating interesting and engaging works based on the cityscape of Fargo." I cringe at the stab and, after watching the cop unclimactically issue a ticket, decide this I need to see.

■■■■■■■■■■

After all my time in Fargo's diners and deserted streets, the modernity of its art museum is jarring. It also makes me think about how I've so far seen the city. I can't use the excuse that I've been limiting myself to places used in the movie, because before coming here, I learned that the winter they filmed was unseasonably warm, and that in order to find adequate snow cover, the Coen brothers had to do most of their shooting farther north and east. No, rather than visiting *Fargo* sites,

I've just been going to places that remind me of it. The museum suggests that maybe the city has more to offer.

Then again, Carolyn Swiszcz's art suggests maybe it doesn't. I find her work on the upper floor. The walls are broad and clean. Her pictures are bleak. Painted on paper and without frames, they are wide views of unremarkable buildings, proportions subtly warped, set in empty space. Ground and box and sky. Maybe a shadow of a car, a bit of a person, though, like ghosts, they are often lost under a layer of paint. Her colors are crude and dull, as if they've been washed by the sun or made from a mix of haze and melting snow. And though her skies are big and full of texture and obscure patterns, like the one I saw driving here, they feel shallow. They don't draw me in as much as they tempt me to scratch them away.

At first glance, there is not a drop of glorification in Carolyn's portrait of Fargo. Her architectural subjects are square and lonely. Like that eighties computer type, they suggest a blocky futurism that time left behind. They're also extremely familiar—there's the Big Top Bingo Hall, the Used-A-Bit Sales—but the longer I look at them, I think it's not just because they look like the Coen brothers' storyboards or like the city I've seen, but because something in her perspective is similar to my own. Her buildings are from the mid-seventies, maybe, too old to be nice, too new to be quaint. They're the ones you see in alt-rock videos and photo shoots, caught in a time only the cool can appreciate. I recognize that aesthetic, its grope for authenticity, its nostalgia, even though it'd shun the word. Carolyn's work seems less self-serving than most. She seems to acknowledge the larger grief these buildings stand for. But I think that despite the drab colors and empty space, for better or worse, her work shares that romantic glare.

Of course, so do I. It's why I've avoided the strip mall and sought out the VFW. Why I've been eating at diners as if I'm on a post-drinking, grease-seeking binge. I think about what Sarah's dad said, though, and think that maybe I've been wrong. Maybe I haven't been searching for something real as much as a version of it that suits me. Maybe I have more in common with that lost Japanese woman than I'd like to think.

■■■■■■■■■

Local news has been limited this week, but on the TV in my motel room, the Fargo news interviews an area man who, because of the airport closures, was stuck in Baltimore for a week. I watch it, trying not to think mocking thoughts about the fact that this is the leading story—I'm getting a mite defensive for this place—while preparing to hit the town again.

Tonight I've decided to resist the unique and old and go to the places true to Fargo, not just those that look the part. After all, while many smaller North Dakotan towns are dying, I've learned online that Fargo has actually grown in the last two decades. The city's universities and industries are doing healthy business. Unemployment is under 5 percent. So tonight, I've decided to listen to that first waitress. She's the only local who's showed some enthusiasm for the town, who hasn't taken pride in being jaded by Fargo. Tonight, I decide to spend my evening where all the action is.

Out my door and down the street, the mall is hopping. Darkness having knocked off the competition, the signs and lights blare and I cruise down the six-lane streets, trying to ignore their bids for my attention. It is ten o'clock on a Saturday and I scan the parking lots, looking for the one with the most cars. A lot looks promising: seven rows, parked nine deep. I pull in. Here's where it's at.

It's Kmart.

Most of my shopping in the last month has been limited to thrift stores. I've barely even stepped in a grocery store. I'd forgotten how dizzying even choosing a toothbrush could be. The choices hypnotize, fascinate, provoke. Why are all toothbrushes now so aerodynamic? Is there some new way to brush that I don't know about? I wander past the other people, numb and a little nostalgic. I mean, really, Rice Krispies Treats should be bought only at bake sales. The boxes stack around me. I feel as lost as when I first arrived in Fargo and search the aisles for something to ground me.

"Ooh, Bonnie Bell is on sale!" The voice is nearby and I follow it. Cheap lip gloss always sees me through. So shiny and smelly and supposedly long lasting.

"Have you tried the Cappuccino?" I ask the eighteen-year-olds sharing the aisle. They ignore me. That's cool, though. The hair section promises bouncy, frizzless, and scientifically perfect curls. I feel no pain. I weigh the value of the "miracle formula" gel crème versus the vitamin E–retinol complex conditioner. As if I were at Big Top Bingo, I feel this is a game I can win.

Only soon, the choices begin to cancel themselves out, and after what seems like hours, I move on empty handed. I try to talk to a mother in the cleaning aisle: "Why do we need to have our cloths pre-Lysoled? What's so hard about doing it ourselves?"

She shrugs and leads her child away. I pick up other things—tank tops, best-of music compilations, PowerBars—and carry them for a while. Then I leave them in aisles they don't belong in.

Eventually, I make my way back to the entrance. I pass an apple-shaped young woman who walks with a strain not befitting her years. Her black shirt reads: GOT CRACK? It feels like a *Fargo* joke done wrong. I think it's supposed to be funny, but it makes me want to cry.

I can no longer stand the self-abuse. Nor the fact that it seems warranted.

I'm longing for a place with some self-esteem, where people have the gall and right to be cocky. I'm longing for a real city.

I get back in my car. I ditch Fargo. Minneapolis beckons.

HIGHWAY 169, MINNESOTA

Were this trip a more quantifiable comparison between the road myth and its reality, the road of film would certainly have the edge. It's got far more points in fun and abandon. Yet this experiment is sloppy. When pitted against the movies, my trip's obviously missing so much. I'm short a sidekick: that person to love and hate and with whom to enter amateur dive-bar contests and tempt country boys with our ambiguous sexual preference. My car has yet to break down in a barren dry space. I'm not drinking enough, or flirting enough, and I haven't had a perpetually killer soundtrack. And yet I find I'm fine without all these. Really. I may not be howling my way across the country—it's much serener than that—but nor am I continually wanting the road experience I've seen on-screen.

Against this, I harbor only one exception: What I wouldn't give to have my personal music director.

Sometimes I nail it. I'm in some scene—sliding past a crop field harnessed with sprinklers, or coming up on some small inky lake—and I've got something on—an old R&B track or The Pixies or some mopey blues—and it seems the music was made for it. Back when I was making my way through the North Dakota Badlands, the earth ripped craggy and snarled, my speakers seeped a perfect throbbing bass. I remember the free jazz that took to Montana's mountains, the dainty Oregonian town that weirdly clicked with seventies cock rock. On those occasions, the music becomes more than mere sound. Like a soundtrack, it morphs into something more physical, exposing a layer of the land I previously couldn't see.

But then there are those opposite moments when everything I try is all wrong. Too whiny or mean or limp, the music can feel as forced as a first date trying too hard. My friends' mixed tapes have long since lost that what-comes-next buzz. My favorite songs suddenly sound insincere and flat, as if instruments have upped and gone missing. I struggle with new frequencies in hopes that the radio will breathe new life, only to hear the same overplayed pop and vacant prattle. There's silence, but I've never been its biggest fan, and I can't help but think there is some music out there

I'm missing that could make this, each, moment climactic. The music felt so good an hour before; the lull now feels as blank as a bad kiss, as empty as wasted time.

Driving through Minnesota, nearing the Twin Cities, though, I'm in high spirits and search for a tune to celebrate. I flap through the pages of my CDs, considering what music the place deserves. Portishead comes out—they were used in my Fargo gloom—and I snap in Prince, Minneapolis's own native son. The music starts with a slow thump and then kicks in hard, taking me along. If I have any pretense of cool, I've always been able to abandon it when I'm alone in my car. My voice squeals with Prince's. I dance as much as my car seat will allow, as if I were in some dim, beat-heavy club just before closing, not in this Suzuki Sidekick in Minnesota a solid hour before noon. Passing a Volvo, I notice a pair of preteen girls in the back seat, looking at me, laughing. I pretend they are laughing with me, rather than at my expense, and keep going.

Alas, once I start my crawl through the streets of Minneapolis's suburbs, the music goes awry, the horn section needing more space than that allowed by stoplights and traffic. I dare the radio for the first time since Wyoming, predicting the typical chase of a good tune's last minute.

The static hisses and spits. A beat of hip-hop. A guttural scream of punk.

Like a hatching nest of eggs, signs of life crack through the surface. English mod-pop. A salsan swing. And the more I drive, the clearer they come in. Soon, it's a teeming mass. Soul and oldies and eighties rock and talk radio and fusions in between. They go straight to my head, and I'm switching through them like a druggie who can't get enough.

I'm in a city. A real one. I'm so fucking psyched.

CHAPTER SIX

Purple Rain

"Baby, I'm a star."

[PRINCE, PURPLE RAIN]

The Minneapolis hostel is a large converted house, drafty with dark wood details. The specifics of each hostel are new, but by now the experience has become a matter of routine. I pass the guy on the porch picking at his guitar, others slouched in the lobby, a picture of repose. I scope them out and they return the favor. Get a quick tour of the facilities: the kitchen with its smell of old onions and burnt microwave popcorn, the back patio of seventies sofas and untended ashtrays, and the neat common rooms that, like an old dog recently washed, won't ever seem clean.

My tour concludes with a girls' room. I drop my bags and scan my roommates' stuff. Mattresses are claimed by the dead shapes of unraveled sleeping bags. A fish-patterned sarong hangs from an upper bunk to provide the lower one privacy. In a corner, a pair of knee-high boots collapse over themselves and, resting on a chair back, a small pink T boasts the words HOT STUFF in red sparkles.

The ritual continues. I go to the lobby to check out the hostel's brochures and maps and the new people gathered there. A guy of college age smilingly asks me if I know where the art museum is. Most of the hostel boys are of the hippie-traveler sort: struggling facial hair, easy grins, and a sure sense of their own appeal. He's no exception. They're not a type I write off, but they're usually several years younger than me and of a phase I consider myself grown out of. I tell him I saw the museum on my way in—it's across the street from the hostel—and carry on.

I follow with a shower. Wash off the road posture and the haze in my head, the heat reminding my muscles they're there. I maneuver back to my room in a wrapped towel, carrying clothes and conditioner and kicking a lone sock that has fallen along the way. Gaze into the all-too-familiar stack and rumple of my backpack. I hear a flopping rustle from an upper bunk's lumped covers that, at one in the afternoon, I hadn't realized was inhabited. Try to be quiet for the sake of the hungover.

But here the pattern meets a change. I've had a bag of jewelry and makeup tucked into a corner of my backpack that has gone untouched for weeks. I pull it out. I pull out the thong, the fitted shirts, and the bras that go best with them. I wrap my towel around my hair, shimmy into the jeans, and lean into the mirror. I know I don't look that different with eyeliner, but damn if my eyes don't suddenly feel awake. Scrunch my hair into its white-girl afro and slide gloss on my lips. When I zip up my heeled boots, it sounds like a sizzle.

I walk down the stairs, past the boys on the porch. I've always hated those self-congratulating HOT STUFF T-shirts, but damn if I don't feel like it. Just then, a maroon Oldsmobile slows by, "Hey, baby, looking good," and I act as if I had no idea.

I've actually been surprised. I expected that as a single young woman in a convertible, a month into my trip, I would have been cat-called more. I recall the big cowboy whoop I got in Montana, a few construction workers acting the cliché in Portland, and a schoolbus backseat of boys in Wyoming, but in the last nine states, I can't have left more than three truck horns in my wake.

Now that I'm in the city, I realize there's something in the mating ritual that I miss. I walk down to an area with coffee shops and stores. The people-watching is like the radio in 3-D. The tats and earplugs and soul patches. The hair dyed so many unsustainable shades. And the boys—they're everywhere. A tall one in dreads and leather. A guy with

Poindexter glasses and an Army surplus jacket leaning over a magazine. I look at their arms, their necks, the folds of their jeans. At a newsstand, a redhead wearing an old Adidas trainer meets my eye contact. When I smile, I can feel my lips' potential.

Sometimes, as I said, my timing is impeccable. The night before, in my Fargo motel, I had turned on MTV to keep me company while I performed the pre-bed rituals, conceding the evening to my room. It was counting down the top one hundred videos and must have gotten to the top ten, because they were rolling out the classics. I was idly brushing, considering upcoming Minneapolis, wondering if my whitening paste really made a damn bit of difference, when I heard that familiar bass line.

Dunk-a-dunk doonk.

Dunk-a-dunk doonk.

And if my knees didn't go weak just like that.

I think the sex scene in *Purple Rain* was the first I ever saw. I was eight at the time. Proud that he was so hip, my father took my brother and me to see it in the theater. We must've spent half of it in the lobby. I remember his stammering an apology. I think he asked me about dolphins. Later that year, a friend with Beta got hold of the videotape and held a slumber party for the occasion. I watched in awe at these scenes I was glad not to see with my dad. I begged my mom to buy me a black sweat suit with purple piping, and I wore it for weeks.

Alas, I grew out of my Prince phase quicker than I did my sweat suit, graduating from him as quickly as I had from Michael before him. My black and purple sweat suit hung in my closet like a betrayal. After Madonna and into middle school, I dallied with others: Sting, George Michael, Al B. Sure. Prince made some mistakes during that time too—I don't care how big rap gets; some people shouldn't do it. Then, sometime in high school, after my friends started playing "1999" during carpool to school, Prince and I reunited. This time, however, I had a less naive understanding of his musical genius. Although I had been long inured to sex in pop music, Prince's lyrics still could be a revelation, and though I wasn't yet sexually active—Seal won the soundtrack rights to that event several years later—I was beginning to get more familiar with myself. I crooned along to "Darling Nikki," sitting in a hotel lobby, masturbating with a magazine. I learned Prince's falsetto screams sounded a lot like how I felt experimenting with my shower's power massage.

My friends and I were also just learning the power of nostalgia as it applied to our own childhood, so, sometime in my junior year, we rented *Purple Rain* and watched it again. To say it was disappointing is like saying having your heart broken is a bummer. The horror of his acting skills and Victorian pirate shirts were an assault on the esteem that we had since bestowed on the album. Outside the disco and hair-metal era, Prince seemed so silly; his effeminacy turned us off. It was crushing to learn we'd made such gross miscalculations of cool, to discover we'd gotten a cherished memory all wrong.

A good ten years later, though, watching the *Purple Rain* video in a Fargo motel room, I was a little wiser. So Prince makes Madonna's acting look inspired, but no one has owned a stage more. I ate up the glory shots: him dwarfed by his shiny purple bike, speeding through a tunnel with the improbable graffiti PEACE, LOVE. I also had a greater appreciation for what Prince accomplished. Here he was, a middle-class, mixed-race kid from the center of America. Merging rock with funk with soul, black with white, a raging masculinity with androg-yny, it's as if he thought boundaries were there to be breached—or rather, seduced, because that's the way he did it. So what if he's under five feet? Or if maturity has only ripened his eccentricities? If I could have a sex life as represented by any single artist's canon, hands down, it would have to be his.

So today, when I was approaching Prince's hometown, recogniz-ing the lakes and trees so similar to the ones he'd sped past, and now here, in his city, I find myself wanting to get closer. To him. To that. A little action wouldn't hurt, either. Back in my Fargo motel room, I'd already completed my standard Internet search for clues to Prince's Min-neapolis. I'd heard he sometimes throws parties at his recording studio, Paisley Park, but none are planned and it doesn't offer tours. It seems the best you could do is drive by or get shooed off, and I'm not enough of a fan for either to be fulfilling. At the newsstand by the redhead I pick up the weeklies for music listings, looking for Prince museums or tributes or events. The closest thing I find is an ad for First Avenue, one of Minneapolis's main musical venues and the place where *Purple Rain*'s club scenes were filmed. On Friday, Black Eyed Peas, a funk-based hip-hop group, are playing. That's six days away. It means spending all week here in the city. I call in for a ticket on the spot.

■■■■■■■■■

That night, after spending the afternoon scoping out Minneapolis and completing my standard aimless tour around the city's small lakes, rimmed with set-back mansions, and into more modest neighborhoods, where black families gather on stoops, I go to a restaurant and bar near my hostel.

I take a table near the bar and sit alone for a while before being approached by the guy working the door. He's got a fabulous body—although he's probably nearing fifty, his abs are as flat as the last two states, his pecs strain his T-shirt's knit, and his biceps look as if they are with child—and yet it's almost indistinguishable through the horror of his Jeri curl. His is a drippier version of the one I saw worn by Prince in his video the previous night, and it makes me wonder where this guy has been for the last twenty years.

I wonder this even more when I hear him talk. His accent: It's not

Midwestern. It's not black. It's not a lisp. It reminds me of that Pharcyde video in which they danced and sang backward and how weird it looked when played forward.

"Heys, howrariatishivnin, an yeshyim jepheraey."

I have absolutely no idea what he says. "Excuse me?"

"Heeeys, hooowraaaria tissshivnin, an yesssh yim jepheraaaey," he repeats slower and louder.

The bar is noisy—jukebox, tequila shots, someone's birthday—but the man is indecipherable. Social ritual, however, tells me he greeted me and offered his name. I shake his hand and introduce myself.

"Yesh, ain't yah tho cute fo sho age, washit yahare?"

Unable to decipher the actual words in his sentences, I learn to get the gist of them. I gather he's paid me a compliment and asked me about my ethnicity. It's a question I get a fair amount, especially in urban areas. People often think I'm part black or Latina. In the smaller towns, I think people have just assumed I'm white, and I've often wondered how different this road trip would be if they couldn't make that assumption.

Leaning his well-sculpted arm on a nearby wall, Jeffrey—or at least I think that's his name—tells me about his town. He says people get along pretty well, or at least no one messes with him—or, for that matter, he says with a knowing smile, with anyone in his biker club, Black Sabbath. There are seventy-three such clubs in the Minneapolis area; Black Sabbath is one of the few all-black ones.

Indeed, Jeffrey seems very secure in his image as a badass. He brags to me about his life in the bodyguard business—"Ishe ushta wok por Queen Latifah anje River Phoenix"—yet he also seems to enjoy the affirmation that he's still got it. Jeffrey excuses himself occasionally to man the door. He waves some in with a greeting, stares down others. Watching him card kids at a bar and grill, it strikes me that Jeffrey's heyday has some time since passed. Still, he seems a pretty happy man. He likes his city. He likes his body. He likes his hair. Life treats Jeffrey all right.

When he returns, I ask him if there is anywhere I can go to hear Prince. A club? His studios?

He can't think of anywhere. Well, there's this place that plays Prince sometimes.

Yeah?

And if I would like to check it out, he gets off around three, and he'd love to take me.

Hmmm, I'm kinda tired. What's it like?

He's sure I'd like it. Did he mention it was a bondage club?

Oh, yeah, thanks, but I'm exhausted.

Am I sure? They got some real kinky stuff. He has his own restraints.

It's a sweet offer, but I pass. I'm not big on S&M. Ditto for Jeri curls. Even if set to Prince, the combo is not a turn-on.

■■■■■■■■■

Seventy-three biker clubs, though. That's amazing. And that's what I love about the city. It makes me feel I could be wrong about those musical highs. Impossible to take all in, the city gives hope that peaks needn't wane, that stimulation never plateaus. There's always more newness to grope after. So I spend my week up to the concert dressing and glossing, trying to take it all in. I go where people gather, relishing the heady clash of voices and styles, the pretenses I feel free to mock because they are also, at last, my own. One subject's still central. The numbers of that Tuesday last week ring from conversations around me, but here it's broached from so many different angles. I read editorials and look at commemorative art pieces and debate with the boys at the hostel. The event is complicated here and, as such, takes on a more deserving depth.

But so far, this is any city, and I've never bought the line that all cities are the same. So, in between the crowds and the press, reading and eavesdropping, I spend my week hunting out signs of that most famous Minneapolis biker, Prince himself. Sometimes as I roam Minneapolis, the city can feel impenetrable, and I think Prince's story might give me an in. I start with music stores.

After Prince and I reunited in high school, I moved on to other phases—chick folk, grunge, vintage soul—each time swearing my current crush was much more sophisticated than the last. In college, I got really into hip-hop, but like many white people attracted to the music but not to the other white people it attracted, I compensated for my color with a sort of scholarly devotion. I studied the underground and the obscure. I knew styles and their samples. Alas, after several years, my commitment waned. I tired of the cyclical conversations about which artists went commercial and who was more "real."

Yet it's funny. Though I now dismiss my earlier elitism by taking pride in my popular tastes, I still feel self-conscious approaching the *High Fidelity* characters at the record shop about artists as mainstream as Prince. They, too, have heard Prince throws parties, but they know little else and direct me to a place called Sun's. Sun's tells me to check out Cheapo's. Cheapo's says to try Electric Fetus. I'm not sure what exactly I'm looking for. Some statue or tribute. Maybe the original liner notes to "Darling Nikki," the impetus for Tipper Gore's infamous PARENTAL ADVISORY stickers. Any hometown nod to Prince's impact on popular music or some clues to where his style came from.

But no, instead, the music stores are turning into a new routine, a ritual leading nowhere. Electric Fetus, like the other shops, has no shortage of death metal merchandise—Korn and Metallica and angry screaming men—but Prince memorabilia is sadly absent. The guys at the counter say they heard Prince recently auctioned off a lot of his equipment and costumes at Paisley. They talk about it as if it were an urban legend.

I get one last tip in a tacked-up flyer for the local Hennepin History Museum that's featuring an exhibit on Minneapolis rock in the eighties. I figure this is a bull's-eye. This has to have the story I'm looking for: an homage to his humble beginnings, a cultural analysis of his rise to Minneapolis fame, and a sociohistorical pictorial made entirely of his nude album covers. But instead the exhibit is a collection of concert posters and album covers from scrappy indie and punk bands—Hüsker Dü, The Replacements, and many more I don't recognize—and a complicated handwritten geological chart tracking Seattle's grunge scene to Minneapolis's garage bands. Alas, I had no punk phase, nor did I lose my virginity to The Ramones. The names mean nothing. There is nary a Prince mention anywhere.

I tell the guy working at the museum, a guy who has precisely the look of someone who could have masterminded the eighties rock display, about my frustrations with finding anything Prince in this, his hometown. Maybe he's just bored, but he takes on the task as if he realizes the injustice done. He pulls out a stack of phone books and asks operators about Paisley Park. He scribbles notes and looks up more numbers. But after ten minutes, he rests the phone. "I'm sorry," he sighs. "I couldn't get in."

I'm beginning to tire. And not just of my Prince search, because I know it's a city and things here move fast. I'm tiring of it all. The city dizziness is fading under the same familiarity that claims those good songs: flat and surface and forced. I continue dressing up, walking out assured and convinced that this effort should count for something, only to wander and sit and wait while nothing comes of it. If I were in a smaller town, I'd take this plateau as an excuse to leave, but I've still got days before the concert. So I keep looking, scoping out places positioned on the ideal fringe between scrappy neglect and gentrification, with the requisite age group hanging outside.

One is a biker café. Prince was one, right? I'm chatted up by a guy who I think is perfectly pleasant—that is, until an hour into our talk, when he reveals himself as a racist fuck: "I guess you could say we get along. I just don't go squealing on *them* and *they* don't bother me." He never specifies who "them" is, but it's pretty clear he's not talking about polo-wearing white men like himself. "I just wouldn't be taking tours of the South Side, if you know what I mean. A lot of them are junkies, here to use our clinics."

I was thinking—or I was wanting to think—that Minneapolis was all that Prince promised it could be, fusion and merged boundaries with orgasmic bliss. But instead it's just a city. Home to real varieties in income and race and gender and lifestyle but also, it seems, to an equal amount of false distinctions. Home to a bunch of people trying to stand out. Styles standing for difference, and difference an excuse for keeping others at a distance.

And I'm tired of the distance, the surface separation from the world around me that I've been battling this whole damn trip. I'm over it. I want to let go. To be who I am in my car. To really follow Prince. To go crazy. Let's get nuts. And I want to do it tonight.

■ ■■ ■ ■ ■ ■ ■ ■ ■

The club First Avenue used to be a bus depot that has been renovated into a nightclub. It's a big black building, painted with silver stars, and in those stars are famous performers' names. Though his movie put it on the map, Prince's star looks just like the others.

With the help of that bag of makeup and the promise of a show I've been waiting for all week, I've sloughed off my afternoon funk. Or if I haven't totally escaped it, at least I look good. I go in through the 7th Street entry, which takes me upstairs, past a DJ setting up in a smaller room off the main venue. The DJ, a black guy with a tank's physique and an equally huge smile, calls after me, "Hey, beautiful, where you off to?" Over my shoulder, I give him a smile. "Oh, you're too sweet. Go ahead. Get your drink on, but you know where to find me." My hips rock as I walk away. This is off to a swimming start. It's early yet and the place is still filling out. I go to the bar. Get myself something tall and sweet. Something girly. Something strong.

In the main room, looking at Prince's club is like looking at someone wearing headgear: It's awfully hard to see the face behind it. The room's been built onto and is sectioned off into two stories, all ages permitted on the floor, the drinkers upstairs behind a large plastic window. I navigate my way among the other twentysomethings decked out for their night out: guys in their good shirts and girls in their least practical shoes. All look to have had a far better time getting ready than they are having now. They stand in clusters like in sitcoms, with an open wall so they can better see and be seen. They fill conversation lulls with sips from their empty cups, stab their straws at the ice, waiting for the show to start, or for liquid courage to work its magic, or for someone cute and more forward to get the evening off already.

I watch and watch, doing my own straw-fidget. I finish my drink and get another, as much for the activity of waiting by the bar as for the hope of regaining the buzz I came in with. I trade a few brief smiles but everyone seems to be with someone. It's like the city at its worst: looking, judging, more distance. I eye some guys down the bar. If only they'd throw me a line. If only they knew how responsive I'd be.

"Aren't you looking good tonight."

I turn to the speaker. He's of mixed race—some black, some white, maybe some Asian. He has neat cornrows, unreasonably green eyes, and cheekbones that could hurt someone. Immediately, I pin him as way too pretty and just as smooth.

"I'm Toussant."

But his attention has got me sassy again. "What the hell kind of name is that?"

He laughs it off. "And I suppose you got one that's better?"

We swap the initial coordinates of name, home, and knowledge of the band. Engage in small talk weighed heavy with flirtation and faked attitude.

"Well, Toussant, aren't you going to buy me a drink?"

"Oh, it's like that, then?" he says with a smile.

"Sure is," I say, returning one.

I'm not sure why I asked for a cocktail, because by the time I'm holding it, I'm very much feeling the last two, the combinations of colors and sounds morphing into a most fantastic video with me as its center. Toussant introduces me to his friend from Detroit, whose name I either don't catch or lose along the way. They toss me compliments about how cool my trip is, and I infer how cool I am, and I can't tell whether I'm alcohol drunk or ego drunk, nor do I care, because I feel so good. I feel like a fucking star.

By the time Black Eyed Peas come out, the ground is light and time is fast and I want to go downstairs to dance. More of me, however, wants to hook up. I watch the band, considering my options. Detroit is surely the better catch, shorter and sullen and not nearly so charming, but Toussant has those cheekbones, those eyes. And now this ice, too, is alone. Maybe I should have another.

"Hey, gorgeous, where'd you go off to earlier?" I overhear him say.

A cute girl with pigtails returns his attention with one of those giddy but busy looks and walks off with her friends. If I have trouble hiding my emotions when I'm sober, when I'm drunk, there's no hope. I make an ugly, exaggerated expression, an expression I immediately wish I could take back.

Toussant looks at me incredulously: "What, you think you're the only girl I've picked up all night?"

The video of me slows, skewed and warped. He says it nicelike, but it still stings. I excuse myself to get some water. The dull mirror behind the bar is suddenly mean. I'm really a drunk bore. A white twit. Time's turned sluggish and sobriety surrounds me. And yet, refilling my water, it comes no closer. Half an hour's abstinence and one sharp reality check can't nullify the last three hours' indulgence.

I go back and talk with Toussant and Detroit cautiously, no more than friendly. But then the concert's suddenly over and I'm offering them a ride home. On the freeway, I drive better than I should be able to. Toussant pops in the tape on the dashboard, a mixed tape a friend made me for my trip, and it's one of the better random ones—hip-hop and angry-girl anthems and salsa and even "Erotic City," a classic Prince B-side. Toussant's impressed: "Damn, this shit's tight. So your friends listen to all this shit back in Oakland?" He's turning to me and saying, "I mean, damn, you're a cool fucking chick."

And then I'm dropping them off and I'm saying I should go but I'm thinking Toussant will maybe stop me. But he doesn't. We're no longer a Prince song; we're more like one of Biz Markie's. We share a hug. The contact feels good still.

Driving back, the freeway is an empty fast world, an ocean's black with flaming white swimming lanes, and I'm silver finned and swift, swooping with curving overpasses and through the maze of digits and directions as if their coordinates are in my blood. I can still hear Toussant's flattery. Except that though I feel pretty damn fucking cool for finding my way back to the hostel on a freeway I've never been on in a city I barely know, tomorrow's shame is getting a head start with the simple fact that it's three in the morning and I'm driving and sobriety is still too far away. I pull into the hostel, feeling so very very lucky and so very very stupid and, trying to find my bed quietly, I'm crashing into something and it's knocking over something else. The shapes in several beds shift and their springs moan a protest. I find my bed, but the bunk above me is undulating up and down and my head is turning into something awful, all spin and evil. Before going under, I have just enough sense to know that tomorrow, tomorrow is going to be bad, but not enough to do anything about it but welcome the dead lead of sleep and its refuge from the nonsense around me.

ALONG THE MISSISSIPPI, IOWA

■■■■■■■■■■■■■■■■■■■■■■■■■■■■■■■

I'm not so hot. In the night, someone has wrapped my brain in barbed wire and is slowly, steadily pulling it tighter.
My stomach is rocked with a swelling nausea, and, though I want to let it roll, my head doesn't think movement's such a good idea. A short spasm and a swallow, and my stomach wins over. I stagger to the bathroom—*Shit, I'm still drunk*—bent over as close to horizontal as I can manage. And shit, it's occupied. I lean my skull to the wall—*I'm not so hot at all*—and the fucker in there is taking his time. Get out already. The walls swell and my stomach churns: *Oh god, get out get out get out get out.* When the door opens, I can't wait for the person to finish exiting before I brush past him, shove over the lock, and fall by the toilet. At last, I let it all go. This is *so* not what I had in mind yesterday.

Time crawls. I sit on the bathroom floor. Advil won't stay down. Water comes back up. People keep knocking and knocking and do they have any idea of the cruelty? Back in bed, I'm sweating and it's too hot and every odor and noise is an attack. I suffer through an hour of feigning sleep before I can't stand it anymore and must try something new. Try a shower. A shower interrupted with many dripping trips to the toilet. I throw on my overalls and glasses and pack, trying to figure out the math. One at the bar across the street before the show. Two in the club. But I count the money in my jacket, and it doesn't add up. I could tell myself someone ripped off ten bucks, but I know a more likely scenario is that somewhere after the last drink I remember, I must have had another. Add the one Toussant bought me, maybe two.

I have to get out of this feeling, or at least out of this place. The guy at the desk asks me if I'm all right. Someone else is taking a leak in the nearby bathroom, and I realize how loudly this old house echoes. Fortunately, I'm too ill to be embarrassed. I return to the loo, have one more vomit for the road, and struggle to my car.

Alas, it's not that easy. I'm not even ten minutes out of the city, at a suburban stop sign, when my stomach muscles ripple and then escalate into a full wave. I open the door and politely throw up in the intersection. A guy on my left mowing his lawn asks if I'm okay. "Morning sickness," I say. I find the road south out of the Twin Cities and let it lead me away.

The road is easy and the sky is simple. The landscape doesn't ask for much. Cars pass me and sense starts to return. Half an hour later, by a nice manicured nook and a sign for a historical marker, I'm struck by one more swell. I pull over. Calmly get out of my car. Vomit on the state park. The little park has a picnic bench and a large oak tree and a lawn. I lie down on the just-damp grass, looking up at the oak-black branches scribbled onto the sky. I've got a post-puking rush, the joy of no longer being nauseous rising into its own splendid euphoria. I feel so weird and my head isn't quite right, and, though I can't see it, somewhere close on my right is the wide pull of the Mississippi. The Mississippi has always seemed to me so storybook and faraway, but here it is. How crazy is that?

Back in the car, I drive next to the river, with its islands and egrets and boats with men with their lines in the water. Still, I'm amazed. Being in the presence of the Mississippi, so shiny and big and alive, feels like how I imagine it would be to be next to a whale, astounded so much mass can move. And then, as quick as that, I'm in farmland and Iowa. And if the first small town isn't in the movies, it should be. An old-style sign advertises MOON LUNCHES AND ICE POPS, whatever those are, and there are a steeple and a cemetery and clean public parks designated with signs of flapping ducks and bubbling fish. Everything's freshly painted, and a boy sits on a white bench with his red bike, holding a Coke. And he waves at me. Holy Norman fucking Rockwell. Is this for real? I'm convinced that I must still be mighty drunk until I see a leprechaun-green yard sprouting three big, hand-painted signs: IOWA LOVES NYC. WE LOVE DC. WE LOVE PHILADELPHIA.

The horror of hangovers is that nothing is as it should be. Trying to continue the normal activities of one's day feels like operating under a trance. Overnight, details feel sharper, air weightier; life is vague and sickly and wrong. I know it's an inadequate metaphor—all parallels are trifling—but it strikes me that this is similar to what the country is going through right now. The world turned different that morning ten days back, and the country is still working through the fog of trying to feel all right.

Yet I can only imagine this is what others are going through, because it's not quite the same for me. Being on the road, nothing about life is as it should be. Every several days in different places, I lack the perspective needed to notice before and after. I mean, I can logically assume Iowans weren't pledging their love for New York on yard placards two weeks ago, but I can't register it as new. It just is.

When it comes to the aftermath of 9/11, this lack of grounding often makes me feel as if I'm missing something. Everyone around me is raging sensitive and sick, while in some ways my head has never felt so clear. I'm a step removed from this mass emotional recovery, and it makes me feel almost guilty.

When it comes to my own personal hangover, however, this sort of dislocation is kind of marvelous. Today's surreal ache isn't pleasant, but it doesn't make the world any more weird and different, because everything is weird and different. My current hangover can't jar a sense of normalcy I don't have. It just is.

I follow the Mississippi south, watching as the sky takes on more clouds. In restaurants and gas stations, there is talk of an approaching storm. They consider the subject so differently from the way people do in the Bay Area, where fronts are probable and shifting. Here, it's a certainty. Only a matter of time. It makes me nervous. Will it be bad? I'd like to get as far south as Dyersville today. Can I beat it?

The land soon sews itself into squares of purple and

yellow, thick green rustles of corn, and the sky does that God thing, rays shining through the clouds like pathways you could just walk yourself up. My head still feels drugged, and all the colors—they're so lucid, it's unreal. The road takes a higher ridge—the land's soft quilt rolling around me—when, up ahead, I can see it: The Storm. The south-western sky is bruising and clouds take on the texture of steel wool. It's coming, like the Nothing in *The Neverending Story*, and I wonder if I should find shelter. I hear a crack, but it's far away. I can make it still.

Rain is light but thickening, and the few cars that are on the road are getting fewer, everyone retreating somewhere safe. Still, the colors are fantastic and I want to get a picture of them, the shades of storm and land and Mississippi and all. But no sooner do I get out than the rain decides it can do better. It falls hard, each drop heavy enough to seem solid, slapping me like thousands of locusts, so fat and wet that in thirty seconds, I'm soaked through and laughing. Another crack of light, its *boom* louder, and I'm quickly back in my car. We don't get much lightning back home, and I'm not sure of the rules. I think my rubber wheels mean I'm safe in my car, but what if it strikes right through the canvas? I know being hit by lightning is rare, but the odds have gotta go up when you are driving right into it. The heart of the storm—so like a heart, mauve and throbbing—is how many miles away? Fifty? Five? It flashes a sky-wide strobing light show, crackling white and pink. By now, no one else is on the road. The towns I pass are all dark, closed up for the storm.

And then, suddenly, I'm in it. The sky splinters into great lights and clatter, the colors as electric and unnatural as a box of neon Crayolas. The lightning is so close I can see every hairy filament, and its simultaneous boom makes me cower in my car. I'm scared shitless. I'm also soaked and shouting and smiling so hard it hurts. My chest is thumping blood and the hairs on my arm feel charged. I've never seen anything so incredible in all my life and I never want it to end.

CHAPTER SEVEN

Field of Dreams

"This field, this game, it's a part of
our past, Ray. It reminds us of all that
once was good and it could be again.
Oh . . . people will come, Ray.
People will most definitely come."

[TERENCE MANN, FIELD OF DREAMS]

I thought *Field of Dreams* was a sweet movie. Based on the book *Shoeless Joe,* it told of an Iowan farmer who, after hearing a voice telling him, "If you build it, they will come," plows his corn and builds a baseball field. Ghosts of the Chicago Black Sox team, a squad ousted from the sport for fixing the World Series, appear on his field, and a story of innocence, disillusionment, and the power of dreams follows. I liked the movie's optimism. I left the theater just a little gooey inside. But I never experienced the emotional response I think those more male, middle-aged, nostalgic, and baseball-loving did.

Raised in a football household—the Oakland Raiders, at that—I didn't really relate to the quixotic talk of a July day at the ballpark and a game of catch. Baseball has always seemed to me an outdated and over-used metaphor for America. And Kevin Costner? Well, he reminded me a lot of baseball: fine to watch when you are doing something else, but on his own, sort of tedious. Before leaving for this trip, I'd found the town of Dyersville, where the movie was filmed, because it figured in my image of Iowa, of an America America wished it could be, but I was never sure I'd pay it a visit. I'd decide that when I got closer.

Except now that I'm here, waking up in a motel on the eastern edge of Iowa, in a town near *Field of Dreams*'s farm, I'm no more decided, only for very different reasons. I know it's natural for a trip's purposes to change. But I guess I thought these changes might involve evolution. I get dressed, battling the doubts that have made a surprise morning appearance. I mean, I suppose my images of the places I've been are a little fuller, but I can't say my expectations for the next are any less. I'm still caught in my own contradictions, disappointed if I don't find the place I imagined, skeptical if I do.

But I decide to go to the Field anyway. Partly because, even if all these questions ride shotgun, I couldn't answer them if I tried, and while they hang in my periphery as I get in my car and look at the road ahead, nor do I really care. I look at my map and drive forward, figuring that maybe it'll all make sense the next state in.

Plus, it's not as if there's a lot else to do here. Driving through Dyersville, I see it's a normal town split in the standard way, with an old downtown offering historic architecture for tourists, and a newer consumer center off the freeway, lined with motels, rest stops, and discount shopping—a dichotomy that no longer disturbs me the way it did several weeks back. Beyond that, Dyersville doesn't offer visitors much. *Field of Dreams* billboards and the city's pledge that it's "Where Dreams Come True" make it clear the Field is the area's primary tourist draw.

I follow the signs out of town and into the fields. The road traces crop seams, the land's natural swells are divided into planted blocks, houses fit in their corners. Here and there, small white signs zigzag their way to the Field. Red arrows show the way. All around: corn and barn. I continue until something new breaks the horizon. I have to drive closer to make it out: a ring of floodlights, in the middle of near nowhere, waiting.

■■■■■■■■■■

It really is something. A baseball field, just sitting here. I pull into the unpaved, half-full parking lot across the way and approach the diamond. It looks dwarfed, but no more so than any baseball field does when first seen in person. The green is so bright it looks dyed; the infield dirt is as perfect a brown as there is. The field is corralled by a gray batter's cage and two sets of bleachers, one wooden, one metal, lined up off first and third. To the right sits a crisp two-story house with a wraparound porch, and the sky's got big puffy clouds like the ones cartoon characters think in.

And there, amazingly, scattered on the field, are ten or so guys wearing mismatched caps and baseball mitts. They punch their gloves' soft spots, readying them for the baseball turning in the pitcher's right hand.

I go sit on the wooden bleachers by a group of girls gossiping, laughing, watching their men. "What brings you all here?" I ask the girls.

"Two of our friends are foolish enough to get hitched this weekend," says one, elbowing the beaming friend next to her. Her friend's smile is too much for her mouth alone, spilling energy into her arms and legs. Out on the field, the batter points to the sky over the left cornfield and the outfielders take the bait, shouting back insults. "We're here for the wedding."

On the third pitch, the batter hits a high fly; the second baseman jogs into the outfield and the ball falls into his waiting glove. The players dispense the abuse the batter asked for and rotate positions. There aren't enough to make two teams, so they take turns as catcher, pitcher, on-deck, and in the outfield.

"When Tom found out the Field was nearby and open to anyone," the bride-to-be says, stilling her hands by tucking them deep between her thighs, "he told all the groomsmen to bring their gloves."

On the field, two players skirmish like kids, pushing each other in mock dispute over first base. "Tommy, I'd let 'im stay on if I were you!" she shouts. "He'll be makin' the toast Saturday. I don't want him seekin' revenge!"

Tom bear-hugs his friend and doesn't let go. He keeps his arms wrapped around him through the next two pitches, through the line drive that skids by third base. The friend tries and fails to free himself, then plows forward, regardless of the extra weight. The two boys, balled together, stagger laughing toward second base.

Or at least the place where second base would be. All of the bases have, in fact, been removed. Sitting on the bench, the game in the fore-ground, I scan my surroundings, getting the cinematic discrepancies out of the way. The house is now completely surrounded by a picket fence. I think it's intended to appear homey while keeping visitors off the porch, but it's painted such a fierce white, it reminds me of fangs. The Field has not one tourist shop, but two. They line up behind the opposing bleach-ers like competing teams in their dugouts, a comparison that, when I roam away from the game to visit them, I learn is quite apt. When the producers decided on this spot, the area where they wanted the Field crossed over two property lines. Thus, the family that owns the house and out through second doesn't own left and center. Both owners have therefore built their own shops to reap the profits the movie sowed.

The woman running the house store shares a resemblance with the dolls made from dried apples and sold in the craft section of state fairs. Her face is a pucker of wrinkles, her cheeks a circle of rouge, and her hair is dyed a shade too maroon. Yet somehow she makes the look work for her. She wears her heavy eye makeup without affectation, as if, though her makeup fails the age-defying magic it's intended for, that's ceased to be the point.

I ask the woman about the field's missing plates. "People kept takin' them, so they decided to leave 'em off."

Her appearance also hints at a personality her speech does not. She tells me stories about the movie with almost an absence of punctuation or pitch: "It was filmed in a drought year and the corn didn't grow tall 'nough so they damed the creek back there to water the crops. 'Cept that then the crops grew too tall. The director had to have Mister Costner walk on platforms to see 'im over the corn."

I always enjoy this kind of trivia. "Really? What else did they do for the movie?"

"Well, that field they built in just three days, but then the grass didn't take and they didn't have time to plant it over, so they just took that dead grass and they painted it green," she says flatly. "And, well, a bunch of locals were in the last scene, 'cause they needed a bunch of cars driving their way to the field at night, 'cept it didn't look the way the director wanted, so he had them flick their high beams on and off so the lights twinkled just right."

I suppose it's not the deep insight into the real Dyersville I came here to find, but it still feels like being in on a secret. I'll accept a voice booming from the sky and a squad of dead ballplayers materializing from a cornfield—I'm able to suspend disbelief that far—but, like looking at *People*'s paparazzi shots, somehow knowing the producers redirected streams and painted grass makes me feel I'm onto them.

The people here, too, seem to take pride in having one up on Hollywood. The Field tells many stories of the visiting team's adoration, how the movie crew fell for Iowa. For some, it was love at first sight. One anecdote goes that the director looked at farms from Kansas to Canada before he saw this house, jumped out of the car, and said, "This is it. This is my farm." For others, Iowa worked a slow seduction, initially shocking the Los Angelinos with ten-cent-per-hour parking lots and then luring them in with neighborliness and fireflies. The still, dark nights. The shopkeeper's voice even gains a bit of inflection when she talks about this. "They didn't want to leave, the movie crew. They said it was like the film said—a piece of heaven on earth." She talks as if she were the recipient of an unrequited crush.

I read the stories of how good and rural this Field is. The Lansing family, which owns the picket-fenced house, has had it in the family for ninety-one years. After the filming was over, the owner of left field replanted his crops because "I'm a farmer. That's what I do." I react to it like North Dakota in reverse. I read it's "a place of fertile soil, traditional values, and simple pleasure," and to me, it's just asking to be put down.

But then I walk out on the field, and in my gut the claims don't feel that far off. The players wrap up their game and a lawn mower starts up. I watch a woman and a young girl ride it along the grass. Driving it like a vacuum cleaner on thick carpet, they draw clean patterns against the field's grain. The wedding party poses for photographs by the house, hamming it up on the bleachers, emerging from the cornfields. I offer to take some pictures for them, and they take me up on it. Seven cameras queue up on the grass, each one with instructions. The groom and bride stand in the center. As I take pictures, he teases her and she half tries to get him to behave.

On my returning the cameras, one of the guys offers to return the favor, insisting I pose amid the corn. The edges of the field are muddy. There's more room between the stalks than I imagined. The leaves are edged with brown and rub against each other with a thick *thwack*ing noise like wet canvas. The corn in the stalks looks black. I turn to my photographer and he counts to three.

"The corn looks rotten," I say as he hands back my camera. "Do you think they still harvest it, or leave it up all year-round for effect?"

"It is black, isn't it?" he says. "I hadn't noticed."

The shopkeeper told me a story of the first visitor: "He showed up on the Lansings' doorstep a couple days after the movie was released. He'd driven all night from New York. Said he'd just needed to be here and see it for himself." She told me now they get hundreds on weekdays, an average of three thousand on the weekends. Then she asked me to sign the visitors' log. I skimmed through its pages, reading the inscriptions of those who have come before: "Road Trip of Dreams: NJ–Dyersville." "Where boyhood dreams come true." "I came all the way from Japan to see the dream." The book was fat and filled with different inks and hand slants. The signatures came from New York, Australia, Japan, South Africa. "It's the first time I've dreamed with my eyes open." "Thanks for providing this emotional moment." *They will come,* the voice said. And they do.

I go back to the wooden bleachers and sit on the top bench. The air is mild and clear; the breeze carries the slightest edge. A minivan, then a pair of motorcyclists, pull into the lot and unload. A couple of the wedding guys throw around a ball while the girls pick up souvenirs. The lawn mower sticks to its pattern, and the girl in the back squeals out laughter.

It seems so simple. A baseball diamond. A couple of bleachers. Surrounded by corn. A trite phrase: "Where Dreams Come True." And yet, for so many people, they do. They come here just to see it, to be here, and it's as simple as that. Sitting on this bench, watching boys play catch, I don't know whether I'm under its spell or—God forbid—I'm losing my edge, but this world, like the one inside a dark theater, like the last moments of a lucid dream, is taking even me in. The bride-to-be and groom come and sit below me. He leans back and rests his arms on the step behind him. She shifts around, lying on her back on the bench, her head on his lap. He says something I can't hear and she hits him in jest.

Except. Except for the fact that this dream, it's still not my own. Even while I'm sitting here, I think the movie, this place, its symbols—baseball, Iowa, corn, and farm—they're the opposite of the natural simplicity they stand for. They're things I've learned to register as romantic but that have no innate nostalgic value in my own life. They're an image of innocence I got from somewhere else that, to me, is at the heart of my own confusion.

And it makes me wonder back to the way the apple woman talked—because isn't it requited, this weird relationship with Hollywood? Wholly and completely? Back in that visitors' log, there were other inscriptions. "I can't believe I'm standing where Burt Lancaster and James Earl Jones once did." All those quotes from the landowners comparing this place with the movie: "True to the simplicity and pristine quality that made the film so endearing." Whether it be behind-the-scenes trivia or the Field's shopkeeper or this very trip I'm on, it's as if we're following a page from the movie's own best scripts, rooting against the big, rich Hollywood while we define ourselves by its images, congratulating ourselves for being better than it while only proving our own obsession.

The rest of the wedding party emerges from the shops, and one of the men tosses a commemorative baseball to the groom, who's now stroking his bride's hair. She cries out and tucks her head into his chest. He catches the ball one-handed, laughs, and kisses her forehead.

"See? No need to worry," says the friend. "I knew you were in good hands."

Over to my right I see a carving in the bench. A faded heart, and inside it the carving RAY PLUS AMY. It's not a surprise—the shopkeeper told me it was there. It was carved by Costner some ten years ago, used as a movie prop, but that doesn't make it any less real. It woos me still. I concede. Reality's overrated. Baseball has salary conflicts and new stadium demands. Marriage has laundry and in-laws and differing sexual drives. I could make this field realer—complicated, uglier—if I wanted. I could concentrate on the competing shops and thieving tourists and rotting corn until the illusion was gone. Or I could think of the store's cheesy souvenirs—the authenticated "Dream Dirt," the *Field of Dreams* thimbles and throw pillows—and those missing bases as something else: a testament to the fact that there's something about this place visitors want to take home with them. That there's not enough magic in the world. I might as well milk it where I can.

The groomsmen and bridesmaids stroll to their cars. The bride and groom follow. The other visitors roam the far end of the field, and the lawn mower's high-pitched hum fades in, then out, with each change of direction. I'm alone on a bench, the breeze feels as crisp as a cold apple, and if I watch long enough, I can see those puffy clouds change place and shape.

But for one thing: If only I had a bat and ball. If only I had a partner. I don't want to think this moment is incomplete, but I can't help it. The carved heart sits to my right. If only I could choose which magic to believe.

CHICAGO, ILLINOIS AND EASTWARD

●■●■●■●■●■●■●■●■●■●■●■●■●■●■●■

I just want to move. There aren't so many questions if I keep moving, or rather, there're more, but I forget them and move on to the next too quickly to care. Headed east, pointed at some name in the distance, I track the thin roads, consulting my map at the crossroads. I'm at peace now, passing the biggest, most famous, must-see-can't-miss stops. Whether I'm running after the real world or away from it, I no longer care, as long as I'm running. Towns slip past—I don't know them, I never would—and go with my gut that tells me to keep going still.

But I should stop in Dixon, no? The signs start before the city limits. Bright banners with pictures of his face hang among the American flags. Streets, bridges, named in his honor. DIXON: BIRTHPLACE OF RONALD REAGAN. A GOOD PLACE TO COME HOME TO. His house just ahead. I should stop because it's fitting. The first official actor-as-president. The man who merged Hollywood and the White House more than

163

any before. I should stop 'cause he's the Gipper. The man whose face I grew up with. Waving from airplane landings and hospital windows, all squint and grin. I should stop because his dismantling of this country's mental health care hurt people I know.

This time, I want to stop not to humanize or get at a more complete truth, but because simple hate feels good, too. Though my body resists the decreasing pace, my head agrees with my motive. I'll just have a quick mock and be on my way. In the Reagan gift shop, I eye his propaganda, the creepy postcards of skeletal Nancy hugging distracted Asian children. I'm just getting into a creative version of the Iran-Contra scandal when I'm pulled away by the women running his childhood home. You can't miss the video, they say, ushering me into the viewing room where a video pans photos of him as a child. You're lucky; it just began.

But I don't want to understand—not him—because while I'm sure he's got a fuller story, I suspect most of it is just a slicker one. I explain: I'm sorry, I have somewhere to be. I need to get out, move on, keep going.

A Burger King on the way out of town divides its message on three lines.

CHICAGO, ILLINOIS AND EASTWARD

GOD

BLESS AMERICA

TRY OUR NEW XTREME WHOPPER

Things are either getting back to normal, or Burger King's thought up a new consumer base. I keep going still. Illinois is no Iowa. It's got the big barns with paint faded and chipped into a style some people would pay good money for. It's got the fields of corn and the textured skies and the roads so straightforward, it seems maybe the world can be drawn and divided into north and south, wrong and right. But it's almost as if I can feel the megalopolis of Chicago up ahead, oozing itself all over the state. I pass a kindly titled YOUTH FACILITY, a massive prison complex surrounded by gates and barbed wire. It makes me want to move.

Only it's getting harder and harder to. The thickets of the Chicago suburbs start, my two lanes reproducing themselves like Gremlins gone wrong. Two to four, then eight, the lanes fill faster than they multiply, the ever-widening asphalt a fat, gray umbilical cord feeding the suburbs, wide and grotesque.

It's another thing I've always given myself the green light to hate: the suburbs. Logically, I understand why people move to them: The city's expensive and the schools are sketchy, they're sick of renting, they want more space, a yard, kids. . . . I even know people living in the suburbs—fabulous people whom I adore—and still, I can't help it, I think the places they live are awful. I inch toward the city, seeing only the things that confirm my worst stereotypes: chain stores, drive-throughs, gas stations, parking lots, bored teenagers cruising in oversize cars and no sidewalks to speak of. So I'm judgmental. So what? How can people stand it?

I crawl along, lurching at stoplights, craving a speed the streets won't allow. Driving through the suburbs at ten miles an hour might be marginally more intimate than passing it at sixty, but it's not as if I'm getting to know the area, nor do I really want to. It's about time to give up on this whole backroads thing and escape on the freeway. Except, though I feel the freeway's movement somewhere over and above me, it's not setting down anywhere I can see. Plus, I keep thinking the suburbs will end soon, the moat giving way to the castle, and I am oddly determined to see it through.

But after two hideous hours, I still can't see a skyline. I don't even feel as if I'm any farther along. Everything looks the same. The sky's getting darker and streetlights click on.

I keep going, shift, clutch, and stop, my brain dulled into blank obedience of the signal before me.

Some while later—it could be ten minutes, it could be an hour—there's a transition. In my trance, I'm not sure where or when it began, but here there are sidewalks. The streets have narrowed, lights have dimmed, and parking lots have given way to storefronts: Salvation Army, check cashing store, taquerias, Black Muslim Bakery, some windows boarded up. People reappear, people of color. Suped-up stereos and guys on corners. The ghetto? Strange, the suburbs segueing into this. And yet while I find this more interesting, I can't say it's more agreeable. My discomfort in the suburbs made me righteous; here it makes me feel guilty. It's been a while since I've been in the sprawl of urban poverty—Minneapolis's really didn't count—and I've forgotten how intimidating it can be. I'm getting looked over. I feel obvious. And this, too, goes on forever. It's night, the road map's proportions have long stopped making sense, and, as in the suburbs, I can see no out. I drive on, craving a release from these damn stoplights, wanting just to move, to get somewhere, at last.

And so Chicago goes. Even when I'm at last in it, downtown with its block-long buildings, I don't feel I'm in it. All its signifiers are there: the force of wind, the El's *thwack* and rumble. I've watched *ER:* I'm in Chicago, all right. But it feels more as if I'm under it, the city running on a plane just overhead. The streets are windy and deserted, like a tunnel or a netherworld, and action is like that elusive freeway, so close my chest can feel its vibration and yet skimming by, a sound with no body, a scent with no substance behind it.

At the hostel, so big and clean and organized and horrible, a group gathers, watching an all-star celebrity tribute to 9/11. Julia Roberts talks against a backdrop of candles. The bedrooms fit more than twenty beds. There isn't an hour when someone isn't getting ready to go to bed or go out or returning from a late one or fumbling over an alarm, light, or zipper, making sure they make their 6 AM flight the recommended three hours in advance. I duck my head under my sleeping bag, fighting my way back to sleep's escape, envious of their getting away.

Because I can't. I mean, I shouldn't. I'm here to stay and get to know it better. Chicago's a big town; much has been filmed here. I could go to the University of Illinois Hospital and see how it compares to *ER*. I could retrace the steps of the Blues Brothers or camp outside *Oprah*. Or I could go to Northbrook, where John Hughes, director of the mid-eighties brat pack movies *The Breakfast Club* and *Sixteen Candles,* grew up and later filmed most of his movies.

Which is where I should go, right? Because while Chicago is a city that I think of as thick and complex, Northbrook, it's the suburbs. And while Hughes's movies aren't as antisuburban as, say, *American Beauty* or *Heathers* or others that have come since, his portrait of miserable suburban teen life, of the trappings of high school social codes and parental expectations, must have helped shape my phobia of them. Yeah, they're shitty years regardless. I'm probably being unfair. And if I know this, if I know I judge the suburbs largely because so many films have given me permission to, I should visit them, because the whole point of this trip is to fight past those feelings, isn't it?

I try to placate my need to move by going for a run: by the lakes, against the wind, with the masses, trying to stay put. Over coffee, I re-study the city maps, skimming over the Royal Mile and Wrigley Field and the Chicago Harbor. And then I make my way back out, through Lincoln Park and the city's hub, where it seems things happen, back through the inch and crawl, out to the suburbs. I immediately wonder why I bothered. Even though I'm now here to concentrate on the differences, I still can't make them out. Roads are full but the few public spaces are vacant. Billboards on the main thoroughfare offer NYC Fame, an out. At Glenbrook North High School, where parts of the venerable *Breakfast Club* were filmed, some kids play soccer. Sitting in my car, I feel like a stalker. Maybe I should go watch. Maybe I should try to talk to one of their moms. Maybe I should just go.

John Hughes is from Northbrook; he himself went to Glenbrook North High School. Not to champion Hollywood's realism, but most of these disgruntled screenplays were written by people who grew up in the suburbs. There must be some truth in them, more truth, at least, than I'm going to uncover. I don't know this place. I won't know it after an hour of watching soccer, a day of loitering at its malls. I wouldn't come close even if I suffered through a week here. The suburbs are too big and closed, and why bother? *ER*'s actually filmed in Los Angeles, most of the Chicago I've seen is actually just a soundstage, and I needn't be any more loyal.

Plus, I've watched the movies: I can guess the lessons I need to learn. Suburbs are not necessarily evil. Plus, being a teenager just sucks, no matter where you are. The moral is a matter of course. I can scold my prejudices without having to stick around.

So I don't. I start the long push back into the city when an on-ramp offers an opening. I take it. The freeway is glorious. Downtown's stunning, the buildings striking now that I'm on their level. I speed south, then due east, at last out from under Chicago's weight and maze. On my right stand the Southside's projects, the urban alternative to suburban sprawl. They're huge sky-rises cast in concrete. Vast vertical blocks, prisonlike, inhumane, hard. Even in daylight, from the safe distance of the freeway, they send a literal chill down my neck. Oh, there's another one: The suburb is in me, too.

I speed until I'm out of the state. Until the city subsides and the smaller roads are free for me again. Into Indiana, past signs for sand dunes and lake views, past gas stations and antique shops, I'm comfortable slowing once other forces aren't stopping me. On and on, I drive until I find the visual quiet I never before thought my style. Until I can hear my wandering voice again, wondering if truck drivers can feel one of their tires stripping off and what it would be like to live in whatever small town I'm passing. And why it is all the cars around me have names such as Pathfinder and Blazer and Ram and mine is called a Sidekick? You'd think Suzuki could've come up with something a little less diminutive. In the sky, homing pigeons do laps, their bodies angling at the same moment, disappearing like a knife turned on its side, then turning back, black and bodied again. At a red light somewhere midstate, I come to a stop. A horse and buggy cross on their green. I click my left blinker and follow.

I sometimes wonder if I've indeed loaded my trip; if it wouldn't have been better if I went to places with a clean slate, rather than those that begged comparisons. But then I find myself here, at a pay phone in Shipshewana. In my urge to leave the city, I seem to have left my credit card at a Chicago gas station. I'm explaining to my credit card company that, no, I did not buy $300 worth of gas in the last four hours, while on my right, two girls get out of an Amish carriage. They wear blue skirts and white caps that look like napkin bonnets, and yes, it bores me to say it, but I think of Kelly McGillis. Of Harrison Ford. Besides an article I once read about Amish teens' drug use, *Witness* is all I know about the Amish, and as I look at the girls, I wonder if they've seen it and if they have, if they too were rooting for McGillis and Ford to go all the way.

The thought's a consolation because maybe I couldn't

have done this any better; there are no such clean slates. It's a frustration for the same reason. I'm unable to see things fresh or on their own, and that strikes me as sort of sad.

I cancel my credit card, find a room, and go into the town of Shipshewana to eat. The authentic Amish restaurant recommended to me by the hotel owner has too many fancy cars outside. I go to the one that sells ice cream and hot dogs instead, taking the half dozen horse and buggies outside as a good sign, still figuring the real Shipshewana is not the one that advertises itself as such. Inside, the restaurant is about half tourist, half Amish. The tourists are hatless and wear bright colors. They sit in smiling clusters, looking around, having an Experience. The Amish are, well, in Amish outfits, the women with their hair tied back in white caps and the men in black brimmed hats and scraggly beards. They sit with their families, having dinner. The teenage guys are clean shaven and opt for ski caps—even the Amish have got their cliques of cool—and the girls working the counter take orders loudly and rush as if they're annoyed. They act, save their outfits, like any other teenagers. Watching them reminds me that the main reason I can't see things fresh is that I'm not fifteen anymore. That's not so sad.

The next morning, on another run, I pad along the sides of Shipshewana's roads, past the quilt stores and doll shops, around the horseshit. The run doesn't settle me. Back at my room, I shower and pack my bags. The motel's too expensive, it's Sunday, so all the shops are closed, and even if this place were on my itinerary, I doubt an Amish family is about to take me in, show me around, give me the dirt. After one mere night, I leave Shipshewana: I don't know it, I never would. I go guilt free and I keep going still.

I shoot east across the rest of Indiana, around Toledo and into Ohio. Ever since I crossed the Mississippi, the land's been getting more crowded and it annoys me. My map's green dots promise a scenic route next to Lake Michigan but, following them, I find the lakefront is claimed by private property. I'm right next to one of the Great Lakes, those strange sky-blue birthmarks I've always wondered about on U.S. maps, and yet I can't even see the water. Damn developments. Damn 'burbs.

I try south, where the map is less stained with town names, and wind into the twists of eastern Pennsylvania's mountains. A meal here. A hostel there. Another run and then back in the car through the trees and hills, winding my way up and away. The road is not fast, but as long as I can move—a shark, water through my gills—I don't care. The trees are thick and their leaves are starting to turn. Splashes of gold and red are whipped in the wind, in the wake of my car, raining around me. I come up on an RV pulling a Suzuki Sidekick with a sign in its rear window: I GO WHERE I'M TOWED TO. Offended, my car speeds past it. I navigate the road's rare meat, the loose bloody heaps of deer and raccoon, others as stiff and whole as furniture. I just drive. It feeds me and cleans me and moves me east more.

CHAPTER EIGHT

Cheers

DIANE:
The opposite of love is not hate.
It's indifference.

SAM:
Well, whatever, I don't care.

[CHEERS]

I continue north and east, up through Buffalo and across Massachu-
setts. In late September, the trees have begun their show. The forests
are blushed red in patches, raw green in others. I take the curves slow
and pull over at vistas, halfway tempted to park for a season, watch the
trees through their fall. But then I see a sign for Boston and it eggs me

forward. Boston, the end of my eastward route. As I near the city, I feel as if I were looking down on my piece on a board game. Buildings go by me, the road continues under, but it all seems as abstract as the map I've crossed. SECOND RIGHT TO BOSTON: I'm amazed to be so close to a word so far from home.

Coming into Boston also gives me a chance to regain my footing. I've enjoyed the road since Shipshewana—the speed, the ease—but the drifting has started to leave me lost. For all my battles with my trip's original purpose, I miss its anchor, and Boston seems like a good place to reconnect with it. Back in high school, after all, I spent many Thursday nights with *Cheers*, the long-running sitcom about a Boston pub and the mix of people who hung out there. The city also has the less seminal but thematically similar *Good Will Hunting*, the 1997 movie about a South Boston math prodigy. I thought it telling that these shows mixed into the standard love story larger threads on the relationship between blue-collar and academic America. Boston has a historically large working class and a ton of universities. Maybe these issues held unique weight here.

Yet they were also prime-time comedies, scripts by twenty-five-year-olds. The cross-cultural romance was necessary for sexual tension. The class conflict was a plot device. Even if rendered well, these were more Hollywood than Boston, and I somehow hope that in seeing the city for myself, I still might suss out some of the show and the film's faults.

As I get into the thick of the city, I feel the buzz. Everyone is leaving somewhere, going elsewhere, doing everything, after something. I'm motivated by all the action, excited to get back to task.

■■■■■■■■■

Patrick hands me roses. They are wrapped in plastic and have a green cap at the end to keep them fresh.

"Oh, that was really unnecessary," I say as I take them.

"I wanted to." He looks at me, and I at the flowers.

"Well, thanks. That was sweet."

I put Patrick in his later thirties. He's dark brown, with round glasses and a neat appearance. Actually, his sweater has bleach stains and is frayed at the shoulder, the collared shirt under it worn from wash, but he wears it such that it takes a while to see. I met him earlier in the day while taking a break from wandering around Harvard Square. His table at the coffee shop was the only one that had room. He told me he was originally from the Caribbean, had lived in Boston for the last twenty years, and worked at one of the universities. Later, when he invited me to dinner and a tour, I was game.

At his car, he opens the door for me. I put the roses on the dash of his car and open his door lock. He smiles as if it's a sign.

"So how many days has it been since you first arrived in Boston? And are you finding it accommodating?" Patrick's accent is subtly lilting.

"I've been here two days. It's been okay." We drive away from Cambridge, toward central Boston. I watch Patrick's patience with the evening traffic as he points out the different colleges: Harvard, MIT, Tufts, and Simmons, where he got his graduate degree. I've spent these last two days driving and walking and searching the same area, but it's different being led by someone else. I lose my sense of direction the way you can in a passenger seat, looking at the city's neighborhoods but not at how they fit together. He points out where the Boston Massacre took place, where a Kennedy lived, a place for good sushi.

"There is the awning of the Bull & Finch Pub. It is the bar the television show *Cheers* was based on. I have not been, but I hear it is the most popular tourist destination in Boston."

I haven't told Patrick about my trip yet, and my admission is sheepish: "Yeah, I actually went the first night I got into town."

■■■■■■■■■■

I went right after checking into a hostel, sure it would be a tourist trap—nothing like *Cheers* and nothing like Boston—but obligated just the same. I approached its stairs skeptically, every flaw of my trip's premise instantly resurgent, and I descended them, unexpectedly thrilled. In the show's eleven years on the air, not counting those in syndication, I'd watched a lot of regulars walk into that bar, and approaching it myself—

concrete wall on my left, the stained glass window waist-high on my right—I felt as if I was at a portal to a familiar, friendly world.

Alas, once I opened the door, it was as I knew it would be. People crammed and posed by the Tecumseh wooden Indian statue by the door, and a guy at the host stand wearing a Cheers shirt and headphones talked table numbers into the attached microphone like a Secret Service member whose career had taken a turn for the worse. I navigated the space, a smidgen the size of the one on TV, and found an empty barstool in the small back room converted to seat more diners. The bartenders confirmed my suspicions: Not only was this bar not someplace a local postal worker would stop to catch a beer—it was in one of the richest real estate areas of Boston—it was also a place where no one would know your name.

"Hell, I barely know his," said the young bartender to his coworker behind the bar. While mixing drinks, he also told me that, contrary to my belief that *Cheers* was born from this city, its placement here was actually arbitrary. The pilot was to star an ex–football player in an Anaheim bar, but when the star dropped out and Ted Danson replaced him, they changed it to fit his physique. The bartender poured me the cocktails' overflow and explained that the Bull & Finch was used as a model later on. So I ordered—a Sam Adams lager, a cup of Boston baked beans, finishing with a slice of Boston cream pie. In the belly of the beast, I decided I might as well go all out.

"The bartender also told me that tourists are so disappointed that it doesn't look like Cheers on the inside that the owner built a whole other bar across town to look like the set," I tell Patrick as we bump down the road. The streets are rutted and jarring as we come to a newer, less composed Boston. Brick cedes to plaster, the university look giving way to more junior college–style architecture. "I can't imagine a real Bostonian would be caught dead there."

"Well, this is Jamaica Plain. You might find it more your style." The evening is getting dimmer, and we head over to a Cuban place Patrick likes. The windows are sheathed in green plastic, and the walls are busy with posters and framed photos. A soccer game plays on the TV in the corner. I tell Patrick to order me whatever he recommends and stand dumbly by as he talks with the girl at the counter in Spanish, their rapport pinning him as a regular. I have a seat and watch soccer. Patrick soon joins me carrying two large bowls of a jambalaya-esque shrimp dish.

"I hope you like it," he says with concern. It's good; it's just not very hot. I keep this bit to myself, scooping around the sides of the bowl where the rice is warm.

"So how do you like working at a university?" I ask.

"I am in administration. It is a job."

"And what do you think of Boston? Is it pretty divisive? Do people get along?"

"It is a city, you know?" Patrick isn't one of verbal excess. "But that is enough about me. Tell me more about your trip."

Patrick doesn't seem inclined to help me with my thesis, so I confess. I tell him about my trip. I tell him about Oakland and Iowa and why I'm here. Patrick nods and pitches his voice in a way that exaggerates his accent. I explain my deromanticizing mission, how as flawed as my execution may be, how fiercely I still want to follow it. Patrick doesn't talk. I can't shut up. Somehow, by way of explanation, I tell him about my friend Daisy.

"Daisy and I always have this conversation. We must have it at least three times a year, the same damn conversation. . . ." We'll be on a run around Oakland's Lake Merritt, and I'll be complaining about how it seems the only thing people really care about is your love life. They'll ask about the job and family and friends, but it always sounds so perfunctory, buying time until they ask if you're seeing someone. I'll ask Daisy why this is such an obsession, and Daisy, who, bless her, has an entirely different set of hang-ups from me, always answers plainly: Because love is the most important thing there is.

A confession I don't tell Patrick: I've never been in love. I've had the odd ones who've professed to be in love with me (emphasis on the word "odd"), but I can't say I'm sure I've ever felt it myself, and at twenty-six, it often makes me sore. But even though I know what Daisy is going to say and I know I'm transparent, every time my reaction is instantaneous. Love's important; I'll give her that. But there are all kinds of love, between friends and family, kinds I think are necessary, life sustaining; so how come romantic love trumps them all? Talking with her, I'm annoyed. Defensive. Occasionally, my voice will even crack in the conversation—I'll hope Daisy won't notice, that she'll just think I'm out of breath, knowing full well she knows me better than that—but she won't call me on it. Instead, she'll raise her hands in the jogger's equivalent of a shrug. What are you going to do?

"Which I guess is why I'm really here," I realize as I say it to Patrick. "Because in these shows, there's the crush, the first kiss, all the fun flirting before the two characters do it, and then we lose interest. It may be entertaining, but in the real world, that's not sustainable." Patrick watches my spoon as I play with my rice, shaping holes, smoothing the surface flat. "I mean, you saw *Good Will Hunting*. Why was his decision to leave both academia and his friends and follow the girl to California the right choice? Diane was great on *Cheers*, but wasn't it all the other relationships that really made that show work? So what's below that love story? What about all those other social networks we rely on?" Patrick acts as if my questions are inane or merely hypothetical. He nods and *hmm*s, looking at the vague, volcanic shape I've made of my meal instead.

Patrick and I drive to a bar back in Cambridge. I recognize more places I went after leaving the Bull & Finch, before meeting Patrick.

CHEERS

In my search for a quintessential Boston bar, I'd gotten some locations from *Good Will Hunting,* all of which were now gone. The Tasty. The Bow and Arrow, now a chain café. Most of Harvard Square, in fact, was occupied by those ubiquitous chains, and it made me realize that if the movies have ruined me in no other way, their preference for romantic mom-and-pop backgrounds has warped my perspective of just how thoroughly monopolies run the world.

I'm glad, then, when Patrick leads me to a bar that doesn't look like Applebee's. It's the kind of bar, like Cheers, that you have to walk down into. It's done up in dark colors, a fireplace burns in the corner, and the round, red candles you find in Italian restaurants blaze on the tables like eggs. Despite the guys bantering at the bar and the group roaring from a booth, the bar's got "date" written all over it. Young couples lean into each other, trying to undo the distance of their tables. Patrick and I sit at a small table, get modest drinks, and return to our dwindling conversation.

"So you like Boston, though?" I keep trying.

"It is okay. It is . . ." Patrick starts, then stops.

I cup my hands around the red candle, feigning absorption in the flame.

"It is fine. But people are not too friendly here. Boston, it is a lonely town."

Later, outside the bar, we walk to our cars.

"Thanks so much for showing me around Boston. I had a great night."

I tip on my toes and give Patrick a hug. After a moment, I shift my weight away. He catches hold of my arm. His one hand grasps my forearm, his other, my hand. His grip feels needy. Insistent. Almost aggressive.

"But I don't . . . I'm not . . ." His voice is distressed and revealing. "I thought we'd spend some more time together."

"I'm sorry, it's just, well, I think I need to turn in. . . ." My apologies and excuses do nothing to calm his face or relax his grip. His hands feel hot. I have to pull my arm loose. It feels like pulling away from a vacuum.

■■■■■■■■■

The next day, after my date with Patrick, on the way out of Boston, I take a detour through South Boston. It's too early in the day to go to the last pub on my *Good Will Hunting* list, Woody's L Tavern, so I cruise the area, just to see. It looks like any run-down, economically depressed area. At a gas station, a guy is showing his friends in the shop his new sports jacket. He tells them about how he struck a deal, and they pull the collar from his neck to confirm the brand. His friend in garage coveralls pulls out the price tag, still attached, and gives him a ribbing:

"He leaves tha 'riginal sticka onit so everyone can see how much it cwosts," he says in perfect Bostonian.

In my head, I'm still trying to make it out. I'm trying to turn it into a key that will see me out of the story I keep getting trapped in. But really, as I get back on the freeway, my car swinging south, the only thing that I can clearly see is saying goodbye to Patrick. I see him standing there, his hand still exposed like a plea, his face caught in a naked expression of rejection and disbelief.

And I consider for a minute that it's possible that Daisy is right and I've got it backward. I've tried to ignore the men who've picked up on me, even though I've seen them more clearly than all the rest. To ignore my own petty, vivid loneliness and concentrate on some greater, vaguer cause, but for everywhere I've been in the last six weeks, more than anything else, they've been my steady. I have to consider that maybe those shows weren't about class or pubs or school, after all. That the romances weren't secondary but instead were the whole point.

It's not until now, in the fast lane outside Boston, I realize I left the roses in his car. I see them lying on his dashboard, him finding them there. Fuck.

NEW YORK, NEW YORK

■■■■■■■■■■■■■■■■■■■■■■■■■■■■■■■■■

Out of Boston, I follow the freeway south through Rhode Island and past Connecticut. I continue into New York, through the Bronx and onto Manhattan's Hudson Parkway. I feel as if I'm straddling a seesaw that won't keep still. I look at the flat steady of the river on my right, the maze of window and heights to my left. I can't find my equilibrium. My eyes scan the city's steel cubes as if, among them, I might find an object immune to the imbalance.

For an authenticity junkie like me, New York's always been the ultimate fix. The way its many styles and people and smells collide has always felt more candid than in other places. As if there's honesty in its chaos. It's thick and dirty and so much more real, it seems, than everywhere else. Well, except for one thing. I look in the distance, realizing that the one object I'm looking for is the very one not there.

Though I've cut back, I'm still watching TV every

night. Like an alcoholic who smokes only when she drinks, I've flipped it on as if it's an exception. Its side effects are catching up with me. Three weeks having passed, the infotainment industry is playing it as it always does, with the same canned solemnity and closing silver linings. And I can't help it; hearing the violins play to two-minute stories of unimaginable tragedy, I scoff. I've watched those towers crumble so many times, I've become as numb to the event's shock value as to the nudity in escort ads. I can no longer feel the story behind the formula, and where in other times I might compliment myself on my savvy, this time it makes me gag.

They say that this is monumental. Sarah's dad says it changes everything. It sounds plausible enough. Then how come it doesn't feel that way for me? And I think, *If only I can solidify this one event, get it out of the screen I keep seeing it on.* Because how else do I know it? If I hadn't watched TV and skipped over the newspapers, which I've tended to do when the only offering has been *USA Today,* I could have just been passing through a patriotic part of the country. I might just think that a lot of Burger King marquee-makers had recently found God.

Thus, it is critical that I see this. More than every

media distortion of every movie, I need to think seeing this one site will make a difference. That even if I am cynical and cruel, that I can make this one thing real.

I continue south down the island, my eyes trained on the skyline, as they have been since I neared the city and saw the yellow lights' flashing proof: CARS SUBJECT TO SEARCH. TRAFFIC CLOSED BELOW 14TH ST. I slide through the city more easily than I think I should. It's nearly October, the evenings are coming on earlier, and by the time I'm counting down Manhattan's blocks, the city's square lights are beginning to cast their pattern. The city's brick and glass and concrete stumble over each other in a fantastic mess. My pulse is staccato. I look to the city at my left; my blood slips through me. My eyes look back down there and my heart chugs hard, as if it's pushing through sludge.

Up ahead, I see the construction orange of 14th Street. The warehouses and meatpacking plants hunker opposite the Hudson, and I turn into them. I park behind a mustard-yellow trolley cart. Nearby, two Hispanic men move wood crates. The rest of the packing district is closed down under gray garage doors, the raw smell of fish and rot left crowding the street like ghosts.

Through no fault of her own, my friend Katie has an outrageous apartment. Her husband is an architect's son who, more than a dozen years ago, went in with his dad to buy a building in Manhattan's Meatpacking District. Since that time, the area's gone sickly hip. The grocers and packers have given way to restaurants and designer boutiques. Stella McCartney opened a store down the block, and at night, with the smell of cow still palpable in the air, ladies in heels await entrance at a club across the street.

Neither Katie nor her husband like the changes, but their place is still enviable. They live on the top floor. Their western windows look out on the Hudson River, a panorama of dock and ship and the shores of Jersey just beyond. I drop my bag and look out to the east at the squares of office and kitchen lights. The length of her loft, however, has a southern view. There, in the close distance, a patch of the island glows a hazy blue, like that of several searchlights turned in on themselves.

Katie follows my gaze. "I watched them fall from the patio."

The glow reminds me of two things. I remember the '89 earthquake, in which Oakland's double-decker Cypress Freeway collapsed, pancaked on itself, with dozens of cars caught in between. Similar floodlights marked the spot for the week, giving light to rescue workers crawling among the crushed cars, feeling for pulses. On those Oakland nights, seeing them in the distance provided a strange assurance: Those hours of horror had happened, they still were. The lights were a guilty, aching draw. When they were in my sight, I fixated on them, and when I could no longer see them, I struggled with a weight born of both relief and loss.

"I watched them from Montana," I say.

The other image the lights instantly recall is the night I was in San Francisco and an Eddie Murphy movie was being made. The street was wet from a storm scene and was cast in a surreal hyperlight. I did what everyone did who walked past, stopping to see what was being filmed and who was in it, hoping to see a little action. Then I went about my night, pretending to ignore the presence of those blaring, bluish lights, looking in on them whenever I got the chance.

"Have you gone down there?" I ask.

"No."

"Do you want to?"

"Not really. The first day, when it was happening, I grabbed my camera," says Katie, who makes documentaries, "and I walked along the Hudson toward them, filming the smoke. At that point, there were all these people going the other way, walking up, going home. Some of them told me off. One lady said it was cruel." Katie looks back at the skyline. "That was hard to hear. But I don't know; at the time I felt it was something I needed to do."

I wish I didn't want to go down there. And maybe if those lights didn't remind me of an Eddie Murphy movie, I wouldn't have to. But now, even more than before, I feel I need to.

In the morning, I start my walk down. For the first ten or so blocks, the city is as alive as ever. After the small towns I've been in, New York is a dervish, the blitz of sounds stroking me as if I were curled in its lap. As I get farther south, the traffic is cut off and noise thins out. Of the few people on the street, none of them talk. The silence has weight. I almost think I'm lost and am wondering how to ask for directions—what do I call it? "Ground Zero" has too much network dramatics. "The Trade Center" seems raw—when I see a couple up ahead pulling out their maps. There are people on this pilgrimage less shamed by their voyeurism than I am, and I follow them at a distance.

There are many reasons we say we come. To mourn. To pay tribute. But those reasons don't feel that complex as I approach the range of the closest open subway stop. The sidewalks suddenly fill up. People line like ants around road blockades, and stands of flags, ribbons, and commemorative WTC postcards are paces from the next. Standing here, in a chorus of snapping cameras, it feels no different from any of the other tourist sites I've visited. And, once again, I can't separate the thing I'm here to see from the many, many hundreds of people I'm seeing it with.

But this time, nor do I try to. I find a place in the crowds, another in the push and flow. Even though I didn't bring my camera—I had it in my hand when I first went out the door, but I went back and left it behind—I do the same side steps and tiptoes I did that night in San Francisco and back in Snoqualmie, searching for an angle to best view the thing itself from.

And as for that thing? Should I be surprised when I find that the actual object of my pilgrimage is not much to see? A brown smog. A distant pile of dust. A piece of equipment that rises at a slant. An emergency vehicle and space in the skyline.

It's ironic. As much as I came here to see it outside

the suspect media and make it more real, I realize I've also come because those media have told me it would be. The news has been full of it, congresspeople and celebrities making the exodus, each proclaiming that its full magnitude and terror can't be known unless you see it firsthand; that, unlike in popular mythology, the camera doesn't make it larger than life. I may distrust the source, but I know now I also came here hoping they're right. So without a shot to frame, I stand, staring at an absence. I wait with the others, paused in this gaping limbo, the crack of lightning seen, waiting here to feel the thunder.

After a while, I keep moving. I move south and around, stopping at another vista where people gather. The building to the right is being sprayed down, cleaned of its dust, and a few drops of its gray water hit my arm. I half wish for my camera. I'd hate to take the pictures, but there are some shots I want to have. The high-rises being washed down. A shot of metal and flag and church steeple. The business-men in face masks, one woman's gold hoop snagged on her mask's rubber band. A shot to show I was here and this is what it was more or less like.

Instead I'm left looking at photos of what is not. The black and white photos of the towers, peddled by salesmen.

Photos of human absences taped on walls and mailboxes, all labeled with the euphemistic title "Missing." I read the love stories and the poetry I want to like. The pain is wrenching; it doesn't make the poetry any better.

I remember when I first heard the news. How physically it hurt. That day of dull shock.

But that seems a different event than this: all of us circling the open grave, searching out the best view. Someone has the gall to ask a cop if this is the closest you can get, and I watch a nearby man cringe. Shortly thereafter, he lifts a camera with a telephoto lens a full foot long. *Is the impact I'm looking for magnified at all through that long lens? Why does it feel as if he is cheating?* Because while it's true what they say—that Ground Zero is nothing like it is on TV—it's not in the way I expected. There the screen was only as far as my motel room's width. Here, Ground Zero is still several long blocks away. Even from a more southern side, where instead of a mass of beige, I can see floors and twists of metal, it still feels so remote.

At a further juncture, I see a woman, her hands clutching the yellow police tape, crying. She looks to be in her midforties and has on a light pink knit sweater and khakis, white tennis shoes. Her back's bent. She chokes out warbled sobs, the police tape shaking in her hands. In all these hundreds, she's the only one I've seen crying. Her shoulders tremble and her hands strain the tape. People are quieter around her, looking at her but not. I wonder if she knows someone in there. I wonder if anyone else is in awe.

I stand near the woman, looking at her hands. Then I stare back at that hole, listening to her cry. Her sobs tire to a low muffle. Gradually, a slow moan creeps back in. It rises in her throat, growing into a high wail, rocking with her body, shaking the tape. A man approaches me. He asks, Is it possible to get closer? I wish I knew the answer.

CHAPTER NINE

Rocky AND Gods and Generals

"Turner insists on the highest
level of historical accuracy."

[VIC, ON THE SET OF GODS AND GENERALS]

How did I expect New York to make me feel? What do I feel
now? Having driven to Philadelphia yesterday, I stand on the
top stairs of the city's art museum. The weather is brisk, and from here
downtown is bright and clean. I stretch out my legs, lean back on a lion
that flanks the stairs, and watch a trio of kids race their way up below

me. When the kids reach the top, they raise their arms and bounce, reenacting the *Rocky* scene that made these steps famous. Around them, others celebrate the same triumph. Whether they run all the way or just skip up the last flight, they hop once on top, pumping their arms at the accomplishment.

I think I should feel so proud. I ran here all the way from my hostel. Instead I feel . . . what? Disappointment? No, that's not right; it's much flatter than that. Watching the kids, I think of how Sarah's father talked about irony. He spoke of its tone, its distance, its cool. I remember feeling defensive about his implications, that it was not my romantic underbelly that was the problem, but the effort I put into protecting it. I still don't know if I agree. I'm not sure my effort to correct unrealistic images is the same as trying to stop my emotional reaction to them. But then, maybe I wouldn't mind this blank feeling if I didn't think I should feel something more.

Near me, two siblings race each other up, hollering and hopping at the finish. Their parents take photos from several flights below. Well, the feeling's not totally blank, actually. Watching the kids, I feel a little shame because though I kinda wanted to run the stairs, I got shy about mimicking the scene I came here for and walked up instead. Now my pride makes me feel stupid. Watching the kids, I also feel the littlest bit miffed, because really, how do they even know about the stairs? They're, like, nine. I doubt they've even seen *Rocky*.

And then, below that, I feel stupid again because it's ridiculous I'm annoyed.

I was one when *Rocky* came out in 1976. I don't remember more than Sly running up the stairs and screaming "Adrian," things I probably know less from the original viewing when I was five than from clips replayed after the fact. I've never seen *Breakfast at Tiffany's,* but I still know "Moon River." We're raised to know that Betsy Ross made the flag and Ben Franklin used the kite, Mary threw her hat and Rocky ran the stairs—an assortment of subjects and objects that go together like kindergarten pictures of a fish and bowl, matching icons and not much else. And that makes me think it's no wonder these feelings are so dull and dumb and bothersome. How do you learn anything from a sound clip? Devoid of context, how does anything make any sense?

A group of teenagers start their sprint up. Two of the guys keep pace while the girls slow to continue their conversation. I watch the boys race the last five stairs. Like most of those who climb the steps, they won't actually go inside the museum. Like me, they won't actually look at the art or learn its history. Instead, they run up, raise their arms, and bounce, their poses as much a tribute as they are a mockery.

■ ■ ■ ■ ■ ■ ■ ■ ■

While my grasp of American history is nothing to be proud of, it's not something I often feel bad about, either. In the West, surrounded by architecture and peers more or less my age, nothing around me has ever demanded much more. Moreover, what I do know has been informed far more by sound bites and special effects than by any real sense of context. MLK's black and white footage at the Washington Memorial. JFK's grainy shooting in Dallas. The soft glow of Reagan's TV ads. I don't associate events with eras; I date them via their filming techniques. I know that the bus strikes and sit-ins happened about the time of Lucille Ball, and that JR was shot the same year as Lennon, because the time's style and cinematography were similar, and I think that, with the help of *The Wonder Years* and *All in the Family* reruns, I have an idea of what certain years were like. Add to that the occasional Saturday afternoon documentary when I'm sick or hungover or the remote is lost or just too far away, and I think I've gone beyond what is expected of me. But I don't know—on the East Coast, this has changed. Not that I actually care now; I just feel inadequate.

I run back through Philly's historic district and to the hostel. The cobblestones and colonial fronts are accusations; endorphins fail me. I should've gone in the museum. I should watch less trash. I should care more about history and politics, and not just by switching to PBS during the commercials between makeover shows. I need to take some things more seriously and myself less. I also need to stop biting my fingernails and do some squats. My ass jiggles like landfill.

By the time I've showered and am back in my car, I decide I've stacked my plate pretty high. If *Rocky* and those makeover shows have taught me nothing else, it's that such transformations require time. Well, actually, they've taught me that it requires a musical montage of action scenes in different outfits, but since I lack such editing, I had better narrow it down. So from now until . . . as long as I can: No More TV. And since I know better than to trust my willpower alone, I tweak my itinerary to avoid motels' temptation. Instead of continuing south, I drive an extra two hours west to a hostel in Maryland's countryside. The hostel is typical but for the several Appalachian hikers staying there, and in the morning, I agree to drop off one of them at a trailhead in Harpers Ferry.

With my car's heat turned high, the fans producing more noise than warmth, we drive over a bridge where the Potomac and Shenandoah rivers meet. The guy, Steve, points out which ridge belongs to West Virginia, which to Virginia, and which to Maryland. Evidently a lot went down around here. On the border of North and South, lines were drawn, battles were waged, America was made.

If only the landscape looked as exciting as its history now. Development is minimal. The mountains threaten nothing. They're barely humps that, from afar, look dirty orange and dead. I continue into Harpers Ferry, through some communities of ranch-style homes, and down into its historic center.

"What the . . . ?" I sputter. Three men in blue army uniforms, complete with brass buttons and bayonets, march up the street. A woman carrying a basket and wearing a hoop skirt the width of the sidewalk walks the other way, and the men step out to let her pass. I gape at the pavement, covered with fresh wood chips, and the full Confederate army that hangs out on the nearby picnic tables. They wear gray-blue caps and wide beards. Across the street, women in bonnets gather, and beyond them one more regiment waits: a crew decked in jeans and fleece and headsets, armed with trolleys and rolling cranes, lights, cameras, and action.

The luck of happening upon a movie set, and a historical one at that. Steve gets out nonchalantly and goes his way. I barely have the patience to park. I feel as if I'm being rewarded for my new no-more-TV resolve.

■ ■■ ■■ ■■ ■■ ■

"Understand, Turner insists on the highest level of historical accuracy. We've hired all the experts, and we're filming on as many of the original sites as we can." A mix between Elton John and Daddy Warbucks, Vic, the PR guy, is all enthusiasm. After noticing my notebook, he gushes to me that they're on day thirty-one of filming Ted Turner's first feature-length movie, *Gods and Generals,* the long-awaited prequel to *Gettysburg.* "I mean, we've got Robert Duvall, we've got Mira Sorvino, but we're also talking a cast and crew of 250. Another four to five thousand extras. One hundred and fifty-seven speaking roles. Never mind all the historians. Turner cares that we get it right. Big-time.

"Stick around and watch," Vic says as he hands me press material. "People just love to watch." I'm not sure for whom Vic speaks when he says the Civil War film is long awaited. Nor does its description suggest it's the sort of movie future children will be racing their siblings to reenact, but I'm still psyched. I find a place on the sidelines. A mother and daughter wearing matching gingham stand next to me.

"Who is he?" the girl asks her mom, motioning to a costumed man seated in a nearby director's chair.

"I don't know, but go ahead and get his autograph. I'm sure he's Somebody." The woman turns to another mother-and-daughter duo next to her. "Do you know who he is?"

"No, but I recognize his face. You too, Rose," she says, urging her own girl forward. "We'll read his signature."

The girls step forward, each clutching a small, worn notebook. While they wait for the man to acknowledge them, their mothers turn to me. "Do *you* know who he is?"

"No clue," I admit.

The guy nods to the girls and they rush forward. One of the moms pulls out a disposable camera from her old clutch purse to capture the moment. The girls wait patiently while he signs and then rush back to their moms for decoding.

"Can you read it? I can't make it out." The moms study the scribble.

"I think that's a T-E. Is that a V or an R? Oh, I can't tell. Well, we have the website. I just know he's famous; I'm sure I'd recognize his name if I could read it." The girls take back their notebooks and compare them, as proud of their illegible signatures as of a victorious report card. The director calls for places and they return to the crowd.

I watch several takes. Large purple lighting sails are reconfigured, a machine releases a fog, and soldiers are given a cue to march in the background.

"The vote for secession is in: four to one, in favor!" the mayor bellows to the crowd, which in turn roars its approval. The mayor looks like a Civil War Santa Claus. His wool vest fits tight around his belly, and his beard is as white as North Pole snow. "I'm proud to report that the Shenandoah Valley voted 3,130 to ten. And in our own county of Rockbridge, only one voted against leaving the union!"

"Must be the village idiot," a guy from the director's crew pipes in, in a voice sure to be recorded over later.

The crowd laughs. Oh, do they laugh! Hats wave, fans flutter, kids jump, and the mayor shakes and shakes like any good Santa would. Vic gives me a big thumbs-up as the director has the crowd keep at it. For an absurd minute they shake, laughing and fidgeting, wild with their historically accurate joy.

"Aaaaand cut."

All the fake laughing lets loose a real aftershock. The giggle moves through the set like a stadium wave dissipating from its center, and I smile along with those around me, watching the crowd unscrunch itself. A woman reaches under her petticoat and pulls out a pair of Donna Karan sunglasses. A guy in a Confederate suit steps out from the center. Beneath his wool slacks, he wears Nikes.

■■■■■■■■■■

For all of the cinematic distortions of all the places I've been, the movie set is remarkably on point. The set has everything: the eager PR guy. The starstruck extras. There's the young actor Vic sent over who must mistakenly think I can further his career ("Here, let me spell out my name") and a techie making a fuss in the town's one coffee shop over its lack of nonfat milk. There's the Park Service ranger pissed at the lights guy for setting up equipment without conferring with him first. He thinks the movie people are up on themselves and disrespect the authority of his badge. And there's the movie guy who's had enough of the rangers. He figures they complain for want of something better to do.

There are also the nonplussed locals: "Ted Turner's got a million dollars in his pocket for every thirty-five cents in mine. You'd think he could afford to throw me a couple hundred dollars for all the income this shindig's costing me," says Gary, who sells corn dogs and sodas from a small storefront on Potomac Street. Since it includes a few misfit twentieth-century structures, his street's been modified by the studio's trailers and RVs from a tourist district into a parking lot.

"You're not gonna watch it?" I ask.

"Why would I want to stand in the cold and watch a bunch of ballyhoo when I can sit down with a cold beer and see it on video?" he grumbles. "I just saw Robert Duvall dressed up as Robert E. Lee, and that lit me up about as much as watching a guy walk down the street."

Besides wishing I'd seen Robert Duvall, I have to agree with him. They've been doing the same spastic scene for almost two hours, the same joyous laughter taken at different volumes and angles. The novelty is quickly played out.

But then there are people here for another cause. The guy who works for the History Channel, making sepia stills its their documentaries. The shop owner who sells old coins and authenticated Civil War–era antiques, well versed in the history of each piece. The sheriff/ historian, exhausted from fielding movie questions. Having learned that little being filmed today actually happened here—it took place in Fredericksburg, but since most of that area has been historically landmarked, they're subbing in Harpers instead—and figuring I ought to find out what did, I ask the sheriff what the town is really known for. He swells answering me.

Harpers Ferry had its share of Civil War drama. Its biggest claim to fame, however, came before the war in the form of a white abolitionist named John Brown. Brown had a noble cause, but he was also a bit of a wack job. He thought that where diplomacy failed, murder worked just as well, and after making a name for himself by taking an ax to three slaveholders, he led a raid on Harpers Ferry's armory to garner weapons for his cause. Things didn't go so well. The first man killed in the raid was a free black man, and Brown and his men were quickly cornered by Robert E. Lee and his troops. John Brown, who barely survived the raid, was sentenced to death, taken to the gallows, and hung. Many now cite his martyrdom as a hastener of the Civil War.

It's a familiar story—I might've even seen a *Schoolhouse Rocks* about it—but it also seems to be a different story here. The sheriff points out the armory, a bright-red barn near the river. With the crew setting up yet another take, I visit one of Harpers's museums. I learn that the old tracks I saw across the river are the same ones where John Brown's men kept a train hostage before allowing it and news of their raid to escape to their eventual captors. I stare at the photos of Brown, lanky with bug eyes, wild white hair, and a long beard. I can't believe leading men aren't fighting for the role.

Outside the museum, the movie is still at it. By this point, they're playing it so quiet, the action is mimed. The mayor mouths his lines, and the crowds flutter and fan a mute approval. The punch line is whispered, and now they all laugh, big, silent, open-mouthed laughs, and the mayor shakes and rocks back and forth like some Santa gone crazed.

After the best reaction shot, the director has them at it forever. I watch them shake, their enthusiasm so hyper and free of context, and I think of those kids reenacting the *Rocky* bounce. I don't know which is stranger, that I equate the two when one is acting out our history and the other a movie, or the fact the kids were more convincing.

I watch for a while longer. Really, it's so dull. Then I give up and go catch a shuttle to my car. Waiting with me for the bus is a group of men in Confederate uniforms. They talk to each other about where they are from—Virginia, Mississippi, Fresno—and what they'll have for dinner. The bus pulls up. It's like a large steel Twinkie, its insides filled with even more soldiers. They squeeze three per seat and fill the aisle, holding onto the handrails. I smush among them nonchalantly, as if riding public transportation with a hundred Civil War soldiers is old hat.

"How are you guys doing today?" I say to the two gruff-looking men I press against. When the bus rocks, their wool jackets rub my arm like Brillo pads.

"Quite well, thank you very much," says the one with the colossal beard. His hair grows out and down from his face like a massive upturned afro.

"Your jacket must be warm. Did the movie provide you guys with the uniforms?"

"This? No, this is all mine. We were told to bring our own."

"Really? Do a lot of people out here keep Confederate uniforms?"

"Oh, no, we're reenactors," his friend says, enjoying my surprise. He explains they've come from all over the country. "Instead of a wage, Turner's putting up a million dollars to help preserve an old battlefield, which we'll be able to use for reenactments."

"They're also going to put up a monument there and inscribe all of our names on it," the bearded man adds. "It's an honor to be a part of it."

When it comes to the Civil War, I've generally just thought that the right side won and left it at that. But it's not that here; it isn't over to them. A while ago, I think I would've thought this sad. No, more than sad: racist, nostalgic, pathetic, and deluded. I hear no mention of the slavery I see those Confederate flags as synonymous with. But their passion is not just for the cameras. They believe the past has consequence and they're trying to make it real. I can't help but align myself with their cause.

BLUE RIDGE PARKWAY, VIRGINIA

The next two evenings are a study in contrasts. First I drive into Washington, D.C., to crash with an old friend. Waiting for her to get off work, I stop at a bar where five bike messengers hang outside.

"Baby, I think you need to come join us," the Eminem-ish guy in the yellow biker's cap says to me.

They seem shocked when I do. I quickly see why. "Hey, bitch, I think you need to get that ass checked," he calls to a passing woman, "'cause that shit's da bomb!"

"Hey, puddycat, wanna sit on my lap and go for a spin?" his younger, brown-haired friend shouts to another. These two seem to be the assholes of the group. The other three—a short biracial guy with cornrows, a baby-faced Latino, and another white guy with a pulled-low ski cap— provide the occasional encouragement, but they're mostly silent as the two Type As catcall and talk shit, bitching about the Pakistani crackheads, what fat Jewish girl they're gonna fuck, those flaming fags, and how the prick-sucking pigs are always on their fucking back. They tell me Virginia's the most fascist state outside of Texas, and D.C. is as bad as a frigid bitch, but at least business is good, 'cause there's a fuckload of government shit to deliver and no fucking hills.

Within sight, a man in a suit accidentally knocks over and puts back up a bike leaning on his parking meter.

"Hey, bullshit-yuppie-fucking-scum, are you fucking with my fucking bike?" my friend in the yellow cap inquires.

"Chill, dude. I put it back."

"Fuck you, motherfucking asshole, you fucking suits have no fucking respect. Are you gonna check if you fucking broke my shit? Are you gonna fucking apologize?"

"Look, why don't you grow up and chill the fuck out? Your bike's fucking fine," the suited man insists.

"How the fuck do you know? How the fuck do you know anything with your fucking suit and your fucking fag-ass boyfriend?"

Suddenly, they're inches away and I can see the spit spraying on each other's faces. The bike messenger has gotta be high, the way he's going off. The yuppie's pissed. I'm not often privy to fights like these, especially ones initiated by the people keeping me company.

"You wanna fucking take me on? You wanna get your fucking yuppie ass kicked?"

"I'd like to see you try, you skinny piece of white-trash shit."

Oh fuck, they're really gonna fight. One on one, I'd put my money on the fucking yuppie. He's got bulk. But the white trash has some scrappy friends. I back my chair away, partly to get out of the line of fire, partly out of embarrassment.

A friend of the messengers comes up. He's a large, relatively well-dressed, homeless black man. He carries a MONEY FOR BEER sign. It's laminated. "Yo, yo, keep the peace, my friends. There's a lady in our presence."

I don't think my bike messenger friend expected the yuppie to call his bluff and is glad for the out. Or rather, I can't see another explanation; offending the female sensibility doesn't seem to normally give him pause. "Yeah, fine, you're right, man. You're lucky, you fucking yuppie scumbag. You better thank her for saving your pretty fucking face." The yuppie waves him off and goes inside.

"You know," the messenger turns to me, "that's not even my fucking bike. No way I'd have a prissy-bitch bike like that."

I stay for a while, to make sure I continue to stave off the fight, or if I fail to, to make sure I get a good view.

The next night I'm on my own, halfway through Virginia off the Blue Ridge Parkway along the Appalachians' Otter Creek, unpacking the tent that's been sitting untouched in my car for the last six weeks.

Though I brought camping gear, I never intended on actually using it. I've never camped alone before. For the most part, being female and alone, I've felt my caution's been justified. I also know, however, that fear's a monster born more of the mind than anything out there, and tonight, I don't know, I feel like giving camping a go. So I use the last hour of light to set up my tent on a site by the creek. And then I go over to the restaurant across the road that, along with the cute old camp ranger who promised he'd look after me, convinced me to set down here.

The restaurant has a bar counter and I take a seat. I've spent all day driving the curves of the Blue Ridge Parkway and I feel like a sailor whose land legs have yet to take hold. A boy, black, maybe fifteen, stands behind the counter. I ask him what's good.

"Well, um, our chili is very popular. It comes in both

a cup and a bowl. I can get you some baguette with that, too. We've got a real good cheeseburger. At least, it's my favorite. Lettuce. Onion. Tomato. Fries. Cooked how you like it. You like sandwiches?"

"Yeah, sure."

"We got grilled cheese, BLTs, tuna, tuna melt, turkey, club . . ."

His friend comes over, a white boy of similar age. "We've got salads, too. With all sorts of dressings: thousand island, Italian, and ranch."

"You forgot honey mustard," the first boy says.

"I didn't forget. I just hadn't gotten to it yet."

"Tommy, and Bill, you too—go refill some waters. I've got her," a large black woman in a blue apron commands. "Know whatcha want?" She asks as if it's an accusation. I get the chili. Later, a hot chocolate. When the woman is taking orders or running food, the boy who must be her son checks in on me.

"Everything treating you fine? We make some good cocoa, don't we?"

"Not sure I've had any better. And the whipped cream—just the right amount."

"Can I interest you in some pie?" he asks with a pursed

lip. "We've got great pie. Cherry, apple, peach . . ." If the boy were older, I might not flirt back with him but, as long as his mom is out of sight, our age difference makes it feel safe. I leave a good tip and go back to the campground. The cute old ranger sees me in.

"Now remember, dear, I'll be right over there, so when the bear comes, you just scream thataway."

"You're so mean. . . ."

"No, no, I'm just joking. We haven't had a bear on-site in years. Plus, I may be as old as an elephant, but I've got the ears of a fox. I hear of any trouble, I'll look out for you."

"I bet you say that to all the girls."

"Only the cute ones, dear."

The flirting emboldens me. I strut to my site, zip up my tent. It's not a sizzle, but it still sounds mighty sure.

I get out a book and fix a flashlight to a loop on the tent. Listen to the trees and creek and night noises. Damn the brevity. My bravado peters so quickly in the dark. Outside, at a nearby campground, people are playing a word game. Someone shouts out, "Flanders!" and they all laugh. I bundle myself in my warmest clothes and get as comfortable as I can without a sleeping pad—seeing as I had no intention of camping, I left behind the pad that would help me be tough to make room for my boots that made me look it. Roll up a jacket under my head. The creek trickles. The bugs' hum is all right. But I like the road noise best. It sends me to sleep.

When I wake in the morning—rather, when I give up trying to find the sleep that's eluded me throughout the night—the birds are chattering. My spine, long used to driving aches, roars a whole new list of complaints. Cold burns my cheeks, seeps through my sleeping bag, and taunts my bladder. I'm tired, stiff, cold, and cranky. I'm also hugely, happily self-congratulatory.

I get back on the Blue Ridge Parkway. Fog falls in pockets. Some turns, the trees are shadows in a bank of white. Another switchback, the fog lifts and each leaf blares its color. I stop at vistas and look at the Appalachians' mellow rolls. They're old, beaten down by water and time and wind. They look soft, petable. The road winds around their curves. The fog drifts in no great hurry. As sleep deprivation gives way to driving's daze, my thoughts fade lazy and happy. I warm myself on retrospective pride—I camped on my own last night—loving the way it feels even better after the fact.

And it goes as I push south. Days pass. The pace slackens; the air and accents thicken. I pull off the parkway and onto side routes with slouching barns and rusting cars. The standard franchises are here, as are billboards for the NRA and 865-BUNKER: a phone number for those against the liberal media. I go to a place called Pembroke, where *Dirty Dancing* was filmed. At the lodge, I look for and find no circa-1988 Patrick Swayze. Get back in my car and continue.

Through Virginia, into North Carolina. The landscape presents no great conflict and I erect no dramas in its place. I turn on the radio, let it feel for reception. It runs through the entire range before stopping at a chorus of banjos and fiddles and twang: the International Bluegrass Awards. If I'd put this on myself, it'd feel forced, but as is, it's perfect. As I curve along the Appalachians, a trio of male voices breaks out in the anthem from *O Brother, Where Art Thou?* Acceptance speeches repeatedly thank the Coen brothers for bringing bluegrass new audiences, popularity, funding, life. It's true. Though I know music aficionados back home who cringe over bluegrass's new commercial appeal, I never really enjoyed it before that movie. And I've never enjoyed it more than I am right now. The music carries me south, into the Great Smoky Mountains. Into the South.

CHAPTER TEN

Deliverance

"Goddamn, you play a mean banjo."

[DREW, DELIVERANCE]

Let's get this out of the way: The South scares me. Despite the Coen brothers' effort, I hear bluegrass and my first thoughts are still of *Deliverance*. Backward, Bible-thumping, racist, Republican. Bush, *The Beverly Hillbillies,* Strom Thurmond. Having never been to the South or ever really known anyone from there, I know I've absorbed the images passed on through movies and bad jokes as if they were common knowledge. In fact, it was one of the main reasons I wanted to do this trip. I knew that my images of the South were unfair, more so than they were about any other part of the country. *Li'l Abner, The Dukes of Hazzard,* the bad men in *Thelma and Louise.* I thought they deserved fleshing out.

So it's with both trepidation and determination that I plan my route through the South. My main destination is Clayton, Georgia, supposedly home to *The Dukes of Hazzard* pilot but more important, that of *Deliverance,* the movie about four guys who go rafting down the Chattooga River, overturn, meet mountain men, get raped, get compound fractures, and in short have a really shitty vacation.

But first, still on my no-TV resolve (it's been six days), I swing by Gatlinburg, Tennessee, for its hostel. I've spent the last four days on the parkways and in the woods, and, descending from the Great Smokies, I look forward to a town's amenities. I'm surprised to learn those amenities include rollercoasters, a wax museum, a water park, and a Ripley's Believe It or Not. I walk down the boulevard flanked by pastel motels, past T.G.I. Friday's, carnival games, and cheap souvenir stores, discovering Gatlinburg is less a town than it is a politically incorrect theme park. There's a hillbilly coaster, and the stores hawk Tommy HillBilly T-shirts and hillbilly gag gifts: packs of matches labeled "Hillbilly Flashlight" and a stick-pencil "Hillbilly Word Processor." Traffic is thick, and the smells of barbecue and funnel cakes battle in the air.

My first impulse is an old one. I doubt the people buying and selling the hillbilly gifts are the ones being called the name. Someone ought to be offended, and, scolding my own *Deliverance* memories, I figure it might as well be me. But then, in one of the stores, I find brochures for Dollywood, which is in the next town over. Dolly smiles from it, her wig way too high on her head, her lips and acrylics polished ketchup red. It reminds me of one of her quotes: "I'm not offended by blond jokes because I know I'm not dumb. I also know I'm not blond." I've always liked Dolly. While a lot of artists labor over their authenticity, Dolly revels in its opposite. Gatlinburg seems to be her equivalent, and thinking of her, I allow myself to almost enjoy it.

I wander for a while and then I get back in my car. For all its kitsch value, this is not what I came here for, and I continue out to find my lodging. I find it in an area that's outside of town the way that bad weather is outside a warm room. Homes are scattered, their yards ornamented with tied-up barking dogs and cars half sunk in weeds. Evening fast approaching, I pull over at a small diner. The restaurant's windows are blacked out by thick curtains. A lady with jowls stares at me. An old man near her turns, blinks. It's the South I suppose I've been wondering about, a South I'm now not so sure I'm happy I found.

After finishing my bowl of overly diluted chicken soup and my slice of white bread, I go back into the night. The night is as thick as my soup was not. The darkness is heavy, muffled. I find the hostel sign attached to a motel off the main road. A guy with dirty clothes and a difficult drawl checks me in. He introduces himself with a sound that approximates "John," and he tells me I'm the only guest in the hostel and that I should follow him in my car.

His pickup's rear lights bump several hundred yards up a gravel road, away from the main motel. I keep close to the red lights for fear of losing them before stopping at the edge of the woods. There, alone against the Smokies' dark mass, stands a line of old motel rooms. My mind seeks comfort in a familiar reference point. It comes up with Bates Motel.

John scratches his stubble, unlocks my door, and shows me my room. Monasteries have more frills. In the middle of a square room sits a single bed with a brown spread. On one side of the bed is an end table with a lamp, a King James Bible, and a half inch of dust. On the other side is a plastic trash bin. The room also has one plywood dresser, a closet converted into a half bath, and an extra door that leads from my room to the one adjoining it. The floral wallpaper is yellowing, and its bouquets remind me of those left at a gravestone too long.

"If y'all need summetin', I'm through thar door," he says before leaving my room.

I think he means it as comfort, except that door, it's no door at all. I sit on the bed, staring at it. It stops a full three inches above the floor. A wedge of light shows under it and from that, the shadows of John's feet. The bed next door squeaks as he sits on it. He coughs twice and the springs adjust again as he leans over to take off his shoes. I listen to them plod as they land on the carpet. I look up from the gap to the doorknob. It has no lock. It has no bolt, no chain, no apparatus to separate me from the person I can hear so clearly on the other side.

"Um, sir?" I ask. "Is there any way I can lock this door?"

"Yeah, sure," he says, and I hear the bed creak and a lock slid over. On his side.

I busy myself taking out my contacts, repacking my clothes. From next door, more coughing. He draws up his phlegm, spits it into something that sounds like plastic, and pads—his footsteps softer now without shoes—across the room. I fill out my postcards, try reading a book, try not looking at the wallpaper, the dirty Bible, the breach under the door thing. It's not as if it actually makes much of a difference. John has the keys. He could just as easily come through the front. That's not much of a consolation.

I try and talk myself down, turn myself off. This fear is make-believe. I can beat it. From next door comes the unmistakable sound of urine hitting toilet water. The toilet's flush is followed by the sink's running water. He even washes his hands after taking a leak; the guy's a lamb. I listen to the rustle of removed clothing. His bed creaks again and his light turns off. He must be going to bed. I lie on my bed and turn off my light.

Unless . . . unless he got in bed when I was in the bathroom. Maybe that was the creak of him getting up out of it. And now that his light is off, I can't see his shadow. I'm in an unlocked room next to a strange man in the woods of Tennessee, a state no one I know even knows I'm in. He didn't even collect my money. Why? I turn back on the light, fit my toothbrush in its case. So my name wouldn't be on the register? So no one would know? For as hard as I try to separate what's out there and what's in my head, right now, it seems a ridiculous distinction. I zip up my bag.

"You know, I'm sorry, but I'm, um, really not too comfortable here." My heart is on fucking fire. I wonder if he can hear my voice over its roar. "It's nothing, you know, personal, but without a lock and, I don't know, I just . . . yeah, I just think I'm gonna take off."

"Ugh," he grunts. "Okay."

Down the street, toward Gatlinburg's motels, I pass the Ripley's Believe It or Not. Its red neon glares at me like a question. What is it with this need of mine to constantly track what's real and what's not? And why is it that which exists primarily in my mind—a fear, an expectation—never seems to qualify? Farther along, I find a cruddy baby-blue one with thirty-dollar rooms. I'm given keys to one room, which, when I enter, seems to still be occupied. The bed is a wreck and beer cans litter the room. I try again. This one is huge, with two king-size beds, and judging by the smell of things, it has been recently inhabited by a great reign of chain-smokers. I don't think it's possible for it to smell smokier if it were constructed entirely of old cigarette butts. But the door has a deadlock, and the room, a TV. And I love it. I love it deeply. I tuck myself into the giant bed—even the headboards reek—pull the smoky sheets around me, and click on the remote. The glow fills the room like lights in a thick fog: solid, stirring, oddly victorious.

■■■■■■■■■■

If taken off the interstate, the hundred miles from Gatlinburg, Tennessee, to Clayton, Georgia, are as nice as they come. The Smoky Mountains taper off into the lower Appalachians. The land gets lighter. Though diametrically opposite on the map, the pastures and easy greens hark more to Oregon than anywhere in between. Once there, I go for a run on Clayton's back roads, through pastures, farms, and soft greens. Running, I admire the wildflowers, the old homes, the arrangement of tree and field and road. I run, taking notice of the gaps in the fence, the footpaths and driveways, all the escape routes along the way.

Even if, in giving in to my panic last night, I experienced a strange surge of pride, my fears still embarrass me. It's possible I'm being overly self-critical. I'm cautious whenever I run alone. I'd probably have left that hostel even if the guy hadn't had the accent. Still, I was eleven, on vacation with some of my friends, when one of our mothers—with what can only be described as a massive lapse of judgment—picked up *Deliverance* on video. I remember the dumb silence that followed the credits, the effort we put into a game of "Passwords" afterward, knowing our next week's sleep depended on it. And even if I can now intellectualize the movie as classist and homophobic, as I run, I keep a good pace. And when the woods get thick around me, I turn around. I suspect some part of me still needs convincing.

Clayton, the home of *Deliverance,* is a small rural town in a depressed area. Its institutionalized population is significantly higher than the Georgia average. Its employment and college degree rates are all lower. Jobs are hard to come by. The local Fruit of the Loom factory's got some good union work, but you've got to have an in, and then there's always the talk—every year it seems—of its closing shop and moving overseas.

Clayton's also on a beautiful stretch of mild-tempered land near the nationally recognized Wild and Scenic Chattooga River. On a ridge above its wider strip of chains, it has a two-block downtown with antique shops and appealing diners. The land's easy on the eyes and the cost of living is easy on the wallet—gas in town runs a buck a gallon and sandwiches at the local restaurant are all under $3, free delivery included. Realizing their retirement money can go further here, some Floridians have started building in the area, and, just 115 miles north of Atlanta, Clayton's had luck attracting city tourists as well. They visit the few country antique stores and take rafting tours of the Chattooga. Inevitably, sometime during their visit, they ask about the movie.

To most locals, the jokes are less offensive than they are stale. A cook at the new sandwich shop has an accent so thick he relies on another local woman to translate to outsiders. He reasons the movie was good for Clayton because it keeps the assholes—"bad apples," she translates—away. A car salesman from New Orleans figures the dumbest locals—and oh yeah, there are many—have got more going for them than some jackass who believes what he sees in a movie. Only the director of the nearby Foxfire Museum, a straight-backed, white-bearded pillar of a man, seems bothered by it. "It's important to have a sense of humor, but when jokes are told at the cost of a culture, when they are based in condescension and fear, they're not just jokes. *Deliverance* was not just a movie. They're far more potent than that." His voice is melodic and empathetic. His presence is Gandalf-ish. "The beautiful sound of the banjo forever wedded with those monsters," he tells visitors. "I wish against anything I could have it undone."

But he can't. Out-of-staters will listen to him and agree. They'll learn about Foxfire's oral history project and its scholarship programs in their effort to do the same. But no matter how impressed they might be with the museum's Appalachian artifacts, or as entranced as they may be with the director, who seems to embody everything that is Good and Right, they're not the reason they come. No, they come for the river.

■■■■■■■■■

It never ceases to amaze me what people will emulate. In 1972, when *Deliverance* came out, thirty-one people died trying to raft down the

Chattooga. Today, several touring groups offer half-day, one-day, and overnight trips down its rapids.

I take the rafting trip on my second afternoon in Clayton. I'm joined on my trip by a Mormon family of four and a group of Coca-Cola reps out of Atlanta, our vast personal differences softened by the fact that we're identically out of sorts. We drift down the river in our orange vests, borrowed wetsuits, and white helmets; we have the costumes and grace of Monty Python characters. We listen to our guides—the requisite hot one, a local whose yellowed, crooked teeth he hides when he smiles, and a female guide whom some eye as competition—and follow their directions on the occasion the river pulls fast. One forward. Right back. But mostly we seem to just float. The companies use *Deliverance* in their marketing, but this is the cheap tour, barely a class three, and everyone save the Coke guy in new tennis shoes is disappointed with its pace.

It's another Coke rep, one who acts as if he's consumed too much of his product, who tells the predictable jokes. Who hums the banjo tune as if he's the first one to have thought of it. On a lull between light rapids, his hyper laugh rattles the quiet. The hot guide retorts with stories of the city boys who come here, do some stupid shit on the river, and get themselves drowned. Stories with *Beverly Hillbillies* endings: of tourists who fish here with their fancy equipment, waving their flies in the air for hours while a local will come by, drop a hook of green corn off the bank, and yank in a fat one. I'm aware my enthusiasm for his stories probably will have little impact on my willingness to camp alone in the nearby woods, on the fact I think those with the area accent sound kinda stupid. But I listen and nod as if it'll make a difference, if not in how I see the surrounding woods, then in how my guide sees me. Gone is the city girl vain about how she looks in a wetsuit. Enter the smart girl, fascinated by Southern fishing skills.

The afternoon elapses in halfhearted water fights and Coke management gossip. Eddies swirl leaves and pine needles. The shore-growing galax smells sharp and rotten. We stop for lunch. Out of the boat, we eat our turkey sandwiches and bruised fruit, reminded once again how like lumpy children we feel. The guides entertain us with promises of an upcoming class four rapid, Bull Sluice. It's the only subject that doesn't remind us of our strangeness. We discuss it at length.

It's all jitters back in the boat. Bull Sluice just ahead. A double-drop with monster potholes: Do people often fall out? The hyper Coke guy asks for statistics. Anyone die? Last year, just three. A mother and a daughter were wading just north of the rapids and lost their footing. Another local died just south of it, but none of them were wearing life vests. On the brink of the pass, the boats pull over on a rocky outcrop, and we get out to scout it. To hype it. To get a thrill.

Across the river, a photographer waits to shoot the tourists braving the rapid. Below, the water's a fuss of gray and white and looks slightly mad. We watch the first of our boats go down, the Mormons bumping against each other and massing into an orange ball in the middle of the boat. Back in the boat, drifting toward it ourselves, we're quiet and attentive to the guide's instructions. Hard left! Right back! We paddle when we're told to. Shout when we should. The rocks knock us out of position and our paddles flail at the air. Afterward, we recount how so-and-so landed on someone's lap, how it went so quick, how we want another, not for the rapid—I don't think—but for the fear leading up to it.

The next morning, before continuing south, I try one more run in Clayton. It really is lovely. And I even think I am the least bit calmer. I take the same route away from town and into the trees. A country-ish song comes on my Walkman and I think of Gatlinburg and Dolly Parton and the Foxfire's Gandalf. I reach the point I turned around last time and continue past it. I run until I reach an old barn, at which point I turn around. I like Clayton. It's quiet. The town itself is a little—what's a better word?—hick, but the people here have been as nice as any I've met. I'm nearly halfway back to my motel when a horn blasts behind me and a pickup speeds past. And I can't help it; I all but leap out of my skin.

BRUNSWICK, GEORGIA

■■■■■■■■■■■■■■■■■■■■■■■■■■■■■■■

By the time I leave Clayton, then, I'm tender on Georgia. And as I continue through it, the state works my soft spot to butter. I drive west, passing trees for which, though October, autumn is not yet an issue. Stopping in a small town for gas, I'm awkward and grateful when four black station attendants tend to my car, fill my gas, wash my windows, check my tires and oil. I continue to Savannah, which is as pretty as its name suggests: Spanish moss and antebellum architecture and so many benches to sit and look and think how awfully quaint it is.

Taking small routes down the coast, I open my car's top for the first time since Ohio. The warm air rushes in as if it's about time. The humidity makes me feel lovely and grimy and young. The ocean is still too far away to see, but the flat sweeps of land smell of it. I pass fishermen with buckets and rods, leaning over causeway railings, watching their lines. White birds make the sky seem bluer. As the day starts its slow fade, the sky turns factories' chimneys into silhouette.

I cross an arcing bridge as white and grand as those soaring birds. Just before Florida, just past Brunswick, I turn off, driving inland until I see the wood sign for my hostel.

A badly rutted half-mile road leads me through the trees and vines and thickened air and to a small lot with the sign WELCOME HOME. I grab my bags and follow a dirt road through the forest toward a pair of geometric domes in the distance. As I near their encircling porches, a tall, pale guy approaches. His blond hair is shaved into a Mohawk, but without hairspray, it flops on one side like a pony's. His black T-shirt has an anarchist logo and its sleeves have been ripped off. He walks with a loping gait and he welcomes me with a strong hug.

"I'm Brian. I'll show you around before dinner."

We pass a trio of pixie girls in sarongs who also hug me hello. Back in the woods, Brian shows me to a set of ladder stairs leading to a square room built in the trees. In the middle is a bed. It also has a ceiling fan, a light switch on fader, one wall that's painted with a mural, and another that is all window, looking out on forest.

"Is this okay with you?" His voice is a couple of years younger than he looks.

"It's more than okay," I say.

"Ready to see the rest?" Brian tutors me on the composting toilets, complete with inlaid mosaics: PEE IN THE WOODS PLEASE. Don't mind the Outdoor Visitors, he says about the roaches in the laundry room. They were here before us. Walking around barefoot, he shows me the outdoor showers, the duck pond, the library, the chicken roosts, the labyrinth, the vegetable garden. Throughout, more tree houses tuck themselves into the woods.

"I think I have time to show you one more thing before dinner." I follow him to a boardwalk over marshy land into the trees. The walk takes a while. Cicadas go on and mosquitoes have at my ankles. The dusk suddenly opens as we come to a clearing where, in front of us, I see the dark reflection of a small lake. Brian explains the lake was dug out by the guys who built the hostel domes back in the seventies. He tells me it's clothing optional and, though it's hard to see now, there's a dock out in the middle.

"I think you're going to like it here," he says. Above the lake, the dark shapes of bats flicker and swoop, more movement than form. I think he's right.

Before dinner the twenty guests and staff hold hands and say what we are thankful for—the hippie answers like "water" and "energy" barely annoying me—and afterward Brian tells me that a bunch of folks are headed over to this bar called the Juke Joint. It's a Friday-night tradition. The bar is a mile down the road and looks like someone's living room. A little old woman named Etta May sits behind a low counter by a cooler. Her hair is white and curled. Her skin is brown and creased. When I ask for a Budweiser, she gives me a 40 oz bottle. I take my forty and plastic cup into the adjoining room, where several old black men hang by two worn pool tables and an old jukebox with a handwritten list of old blues and eighties R&B sits in the corner.

Within half an hour, the bar's few locals are outnumbered by the dozen white hostel kids. We mingle as we play pool and work our way through our beers, and then we retire to our corners. I sit with Brian and the other staff, who pay for their room and board by working at the hostel and doing general maintenance, and by repairing boardwalks, building new outhouses and showers, installing electricity and running water, and creating the mosaics and murals that decorate every building. I listen to them swap stories they've acquired here, sharing the last of my beer with the three girls I met earlier. They buy another to return the favor.

At an unknown hour later, when Brian and I get back to the hostel, he tells me there's one more place he'd like to show me. I follow him closely over another skinny boardwalk, over the duck pond and into the swamped woods. The boardwalk takes a twisting route through the darkness, and Brian suggests I hold onto the back of his shirt so I don't misstep. Feeling the beer, I take him up on it, clutching his hem until we come to a hexagonal glass structure built on a raised wooden deck. I mimic Brian's solemnity as he shows me around the glass house, and when I lie on the deck, he joins me. I ask him about high school, perhaps because he acts to me as if he just got out. He wears his height and strength as if they're conspicuous. His punk style seems less like him than a leftover from an old peer group. Brian says high school kinda sucked, but he says it cheerfully. Brian doesn't swear. He doesn't drink. He boastfully calls himself a hippie but I'm not sure that's an accurate assessment, either.

The cicadas respond to their invisible conductor, rallying to a high chorus. Something plops in the nearby water and I sit up, leaning on my elbows. "Your shoulders look tight from all that driving," he says, shifting behind me to massage them. It's a move his hands aren't confident enough to pull off. His fingers feel about my back, lost and too gentle. I tell him that feels nice but I'm cold, taking his hands and wrapping them around me.

We sit like this, me leaning back into his chest. I listen to his breathing. The bugs. Voices giddy in the distance, more people returning from the Juke. I rub his hand.

"Are you still cold?" His voice cracks.

"No." My hand moves up his arm. His breath beats in my ear. My back begins to hurt. His arms still where I put them, I turn around. His lips are soft. Warm. More sure than the rest of him would have me expect.

A persistent rooster screams me awake in the morning. The fan pulses overhead, working at the humidity already dampening my skin. I can taste last night's beer and kissing. All we did was make out for a while, but I like the way I can still feel it on my mouth.

After having coffee with some of the people I met last night—our conversation lazy, as if I've known them much longer—I head down to the lake. The water is perfect and I love swimming naked. I lie on the dock for hours, the sun burning water off my body, drawing out sweat, forcing me to jump in and do it again. People come out and join me occasionally. We talk around nipples, our pubic hair, and flaccid parts, our acting normal eventually giving way to feeling it.

There are no TVs or newspapers at the hostel. Back at the domes, I talk with the girls as they paint each other body tattoos, play some of the boys at pool, keep my distance from the one dreaded white guy unfamiliar, it seems, with soap. Brian lopes by, says hello. He wears another T-shirt with torn-off sleeves, this one with a big yellow happy face, and he's still barefoot. He really is a dork. He's also pretty damn cute.

Dinner is another thank-you circle, and after dishes we all hang late around a fire. When the drumming circle turns into a particularly bad poetry slam, I go to bed, telling Brian to swing by if he'd like. When he does, we small-talk some and make out more, touching and rubbing above our clothes. We gradually strip each other to our underwear. His skin is luminous in the dark. His body is big and firm. He plays with my hair, compliments my kissing. We touch more and rub harder, dry-humping like kids. I ask if he has a condom. He says he's sorry: Drinking and swearing aren't the only things he doesn't do.

The next morning I go back to the lake, where I lie

naked and basking. I swim crooked laps around the lake, and with the exception of my ankles, which are gnawed raw with bites, my body feels good. Tan takes to me quickly, and by the afternoon, I'm already dark. When I run into Brian in the afternoon, he isn't feeling well. His forehead is clammy against my palm.

The next day I return to the lake, but the isolation begins to stir me, and in the afternoon, I find myself driving into Brunswick just to read a paper. The day after brings rain. People gather on the screen porch and talk excitedly about an upcoming sweat lodge. New York comes up. The smelly guy says he doesn't pay any attention: "That's another world." One girl segues into her theory on how the color orange can bring about world peace. In that night's circle, during the thanks for Harmony and Spirits, my sarcasm threatens to expose itself. When it comes to me, I say it's been great, but it's time I move on.

After dinner, Brian tells me to make sure I say goodbye the next day before I go. A few of the other staff invite me to smoke up with them, a last hurrah. They've been working all week on the Bunk House, a double-decker structure whose lower room has been redecorated with murals and hammocks, and tonight's its initiation. I cough hard on my third hit and follow them to the room. It's lit up with candles, and five of the large rainbow hammocks are already full of swinging bodies. We occupy the rest of the hammocks, some doubling up, others wrapping the nets around them like a cocoon, seeing if they can be swung in a full circle. I lie outstretched, enjoying the hammocks' slow rock, the voices around the room. Someone else brings in a CD player and plays Willie Nelson. "Georgia on My Mind." Everyone quiets. His voice is honey and fills the room as if he's here. No peace I find, he sings. Just an old sweet song.

CHAPTER ELEVEN

The Truman Show

"Cue the sun."

[CHRISTOF, THE TRUMAN SHOW]

F lorida is only miles away. It feels like decades. The transition is brutal.

I take a coastal route south through St. Augustine and Daytona Beach. Homes line the shore, competing for ocean views, though the ocean itself looks gray and tame, hardly worth all the fuss. I stay in a motel that, though no crappier than any other I've been in now, seems more so. Its beige walls are cruelly bland, its artwork's attempt at personality, insulting. TV provides escape for the first two hours. The next three make me not like myself.

In the morning, I try inland routes down. Here there are a few nice crop fields, but I also pass communities that make Fargo seem inspired. The tracts of trailer and gated and retirement homes crowd each other in the heat. I drive by Lake Okeechobee, the big blue spot on Florida's map. Hidden by a tall, bland dike, Okeechobee doesn't look like a lake. It looks like the wall of a climb-up swimming pool set in a shitty back yard.

In Miami, I stay with a friend. Midwestern in birth and appearance, Lauri makes up for it with an excess of Miami attitude. I couldn't have a better tour guide. She knows all the names and drops them whenever she gets the chance. On a tour of the city, Lauri shows me the house next to her parents', which was used in a Gloria Estefan video, and drives me by the clubs Cameron Diaz and Ricky Martin own. She takes me to a famous motel and to a restaurant where people greet her with kisses and send us out food. Down past the house where Versace was killed, by the deco buildings now ill-suited homes to T.G.I. Friday's and the Gap, we lie topless on South Beach and wade in the warm water.

Really, Lauri's a great host. I feel bad I can't stand any of it, that I don't like the city. That it makes me not like myself. I lie, say I had a great time, and take off.

I cut out again, cross the Everglades to the Gulf, and head up the other side of the state. When I see a Salvation Army, I pull over. I think it might help me detox. I wander the aisles, singing along with the music on the store stereo, smiling with the woman across the aisle when we catch each other in the same Lionel Richie refrain. In the casual-wear section, an older lady holds out a lavender sweatshirt to me.

"Do you like this?" she asks.

"Sure, that's a real pretty color on you."

"It's for my granddaughter, Isabelle. She's turning thirteen next week."

"Well, in that case, I'm not sure, but the kittens might be a little young for her."

"Yeah, but she's a fat girl," she snaps. "I think this is the only one she'll fit."

"Hmm, well, yeah, then, it's just lovely," I reply, already distracted by a shirt in an adjoining aisle. It's an old, thin white T with a stylized picture of a Ford muscle car. Under the car, in black seventies script, is the word BANDIT.

Part of me still believes in my original odyssey. I still respect what Gandalf at the Foxfire Museum stood for. He thought there was such a thing as truth and distortion, as something real and something myth, and that it was critical we tell the difference between them. Unfortunately, on my trip, this has been easier said than done. Authenticity overlaps imitation merges with satire turns into nostalgia and recycles back again. In thrift stores, however, these lines aren't so confusing. Like a Miamian with a Chanel bag, I can tell the old ringer Ts from a modern knockoff, a good pair of eighties Op red cord shorts from the new pleather jackets. In here, my issues are decipherable, the trespasses tangible. I check out the shirt's tag and sleeve stains. It's an original, it fits me, and if I make some cuts, it could be killer.

I continue up through St. Petersburg and Tampa Bay, hopscotching to every Goodwill, Salvation Army, and St. Vincent's along the way. In Clearwater, I get a big-buckled belt, in Panama City, a great silver-snapped, flowered Western shirt. The map on my passenger seat is well worn now, but I can still see through to the towns I marked so many months ago. One of the last ones left, Seaside, lies a little farther along the panhandle. Seaside is the home of *The Truman Show,* the 1998 Jim Carrey movie about a man who's been the unwitting star of a TV show every hour, every day since his birth, whose entire hometown of Seahaven is a Hollywood set. I follow Seaside's turnoff and drive along the Gulf.

As impossible as my search has proved, for some reason the place still pulls me. I saw the movie in college. I can't say it influenced me in any profound way. But I keep thinking about this whole matter of make-believe, and how believing can make things solid; of expectations and their inevitabilities; of this whole archaic search for something both genuine and satisfying. And though I should know better by now—driving toward Seaside, I still hold some needy, baby-weak hope this town might offer a way out.

■■■■■■■■■■

Seaside was founded back in the late seventies by a Miami developer named Robert Davis. Blessed with eighty acres his grandfather had bought in 1946, Davis set about building a housing community that, at the time, was considered risky. Instead of the condos so popular on the Floridian coast, he sought to revive northwest Florida's old wood-cottage designs, and the best way he found he could do this was by modeling his development after a small town. He drew up a plan of bungalows set on looping streets around a central square, a plan that refocused condos' priority on sea views into a focus on community. All homes would be within a quarter mile's walking distance from the center to encourage walking instead of driving. The bungalows would be mandated to share a neo-Victorian look, but the architects also designed in differences to lessen the homogeneity; while the houses all had white picket fences, no identical fences were allowed on the same block. The beach would be accessible via a public pavilion, and the central square would have markets, independent stores, international food and news and local artists, creating a place with a small town's homeyness but with fewer of its disadvantages.

Davis's risk paid off. Seaside's nostalgia more than offset the condos' cost-effectiveness. The "town" is now home to more than 450 residences and businesses, and its cottages that sold for $65,000 when it opened in 1983 now fetch more than a million. Its success has spurred a series of copycats on Florida's panhandle, and among developers Seaside is considered a model of "new urbanism." So complete was Davis's vision of a small town that when *The Truman Show*'s director, Peter Weir, had to scrap his plan of building Seahaven on a Hollywood set and was searching for other locations, he said of Seaside, "It looked like it had been built for our show."

I come to Seaside the day before Halloween. It feels, however, as if I've entered Martha Stewart's *Living*'s Easter issue. I'm in Marilyn Manson's personal hell. Seaside's homes are all painted a shade of Yoplait, white porches and picket trim. Golf carts park by many of them, Barbie-mobiles beside their perfect dollhouses. I don't think Weir could have built a more surreal film set for *Truman*'s Seahaven if he tried. All the plants are pruned, the buildings are freshly painted, and the people are well put together. Equal parts Doris Day and Philip K. Dick—it reminds me as much of *The Truman Show* as that old series *The Prisoner*—I've never been in a place both so retro and so sci-fi at the same time.

I wander through the main square, awash in Seaside's good intentions. Across from the pavilion that leads down to the beach is a lawn amphitheater with a small, pillared post office. Arranged in a half circle around the lawn are all the shops a town could need: a newsstand, a café and bakery, a bookstore, an ice creamery, "Bow Wow Meow," a pet accessory store, and an imported-foods store whose high shelves and rolling library ladder I recognize as *Truman*'s friendly, old-fashioned, neighborhood grocer.

I'm actually kinda impressed with Seaside. Its sidewalks, independent stores, and focus on community address a lot of the judgments I've enjoyed making about other towns. People ride bikes down the brick streets and store owners smile at me when I enter. So what if the employees' friendliness is the same I show customers when I'm waiting tables? So what if the town's not actually a town? When I stop by Seaside's real estate office I learn that instead of a mayor, Seaside has a CEO. Instead of representatives, it has a board. The Realtor brags to me about Seaside's sense of community, that it's open for everyone—claims I find incompatible with the fact that more than 60 percent of the homes are rentals, and that those that are for sale start at $900,000. So does she exaggerate the heterogeneity of its residents when, with the exception of the Latino construction workers down the road, the only people I've seen are like the homes, very white? But again, so what? This is the standard charade. The biggest crime I can accuse Seaside of is that it is a planned community and it reminds me vaguely of Disneyland, which, though unsettling, doesn't have the malicious intent for which I can fault it.

Still, Seaside weirds me out. *The Truman Show* was made during the first boom of reality television, its product placements and town-size soundstage a play on reality TV's extreme but imaginable conclusion. It also, I thought, was a reflection on the absurdity of media ideals, a satire of this too-perfect town. But this doesn't seem to be the consensus here. Many here seem to take the movie as proof that Seaside is as perfect as all that. And after several hours of unconsciously searching out errant weeds and facial hair, this simple difference in understanding starts to get under my skin. I need a break. I cross the pavilion of more specialty shops to a white boardwalk that leads to the beach.

■ ■■■■■■■■

Hidden from town behind a bluff, the sand is as bright and fine as any I've seen. Lapping at the shore like a drunken kitten, the ocean looks as if it's found the tranquility all the other oceans are beating themselves up over. The sky is blue, but not perfectly so, and stretches out with the ocean as if reaching for its toes, not knowing it'll never touch. I walk a long way down the beach, away from the identical umbrellas that camp on Seaside's part of the beach, walking until I find a space I can lie out without disrupting parts of my new lineless tan.

After finding a good enough spot, I lie on my stomach, reading Seaside's version of a newspaper. Though formatted like the independent press, the *Seaside Times* is actually a brochure. Along with a brief history of Seaside and a chronicle of monthly events, it lists what it takes to keep Seaside running: "3,500 gallons of paint a year," "6,250 bars of soap a month (we're very clean here)," and "500 behind-the-scene workers, including children, cats and dogs."

I flip over. I've been sunbathing topless for weeks now and it feels natural. Occasionally people pass me farther down by the shore and I angle the paper down just in case. I hear the orange beach-mobile driving toward me before I see it. By the time it's within sight, I'm back on my stomach, tying my top back on.

"How are you doing today, Miss?" The driver is a brown-haired boy in his later teens.

"Just fine, thanks. Yourself?"

"Pretty good. So, yeah, I came down here because, well, we got a complaint of some, um, indecent exposure on the beach. But you know, never mind that. It's okay. You just go on doing what you were doing before."

I tell him thanks, but I'm fine as is. He says really, it's no bother, and wishes me a good afternoon. I can't believe someone called me in, newspaper hidden and half a mile down the beach. I don't know whether it makes me embarrassed or proud.

I return to my paper, studying a map of the town. In *The Truman Show*'s Seahaven, all the streets were named for famous actors: Lancaster Square and Barrymore Road. Seaside's map shows the rental homes, with names such as Independence Day, It's a Wonderful Life, and Truman's Place. Inside the back page of the paper is also a list of credits. "The verbal

CHICK FLICK ROAD KILL

tone of the town (was) created by our creative director." I wonder if he's responsible for calling pets "behind-the-scene workers." Why Seaside's verbal tone is so similar to the movies'. I turn on my back, undoing the straps but keeping myself covered. I can almost understand a company caricaturing a town, hoping that in mimicry, it can sell an ideal otherwise impossible. But is Seaside modeling itself after a town or a movie's version of a town? And what's the consequence if it's the latter?

I'm interrupted by a familiar motor. This time he's brought along a fellow lifeguard.

"I thought I said it was okay to do what you were doing," he scolds me.

"I thought it better I didn't. I don't want to upset the locals."

"They could use some upsetting," his friend offers. "So what brings you to our Seaside anyway?"

I tell them I'm on a road trip and they're impressed. Two and a half months it's been? One of them took a road trip to Chicago once, which was phat, but that was only, like, three days. So where have I been? What am I driving? A convertible—that must be sweet. They bet it's killer out there. They bet I have some stories.

I look at them looking at me as we talk. I wonder what they see. Do they see my cellulite, or just the size of my breasts? Do they see me as an older woman? Or am I an outlaw?

"So you've been taking two-lane roads the whole time? That's the

252

way to do it. And all on your own? Damn." It's possible, yes, I'm even all that: Wise. Real. Very fucking cool.

Their flattery is nice, but I'm not in the mood. I turn absently back to my paper. The boys notice my withdrawal and say parting words, assuring me one last time it's okay to take my top off. I watch their buggy speed back toward Seaside. They drive a crooked line, but for some reason, the illusion is the opposite: as if they are on a straightaway and the beach and I are shaking in its wake. I hope they don't mistake my blasé for cool. Really, I wish it would just mean the truth: that I'm none of it.

And I wonder why Seaside feels so threatening. Not because it's so intrinsically bad but because, even if my costume looks more like a gritty thrift store T than Seaside's white picket fences, it's truer to my heart than I'd like.

I'd call it an epiphany, except I've known it all along.

I fear my own impersonations. I'm scared of aiming for something that doesn't exist. Of my private wishes for a better body, a better job, a better life; the privilege and burden of my inner optimism, how wholly I ache for romantic love, fulfillment, and happily ever after. I hate my inability to talk myself out of my expectations, unable to control what I want. I hate how my never having control inhibits my ability to ever truly lose it. I look back to the horizon, a trick taught to me when I've been sick on boats. The two blues of the horizon are so straight, it's unnatural. I came to this corner of the Gulf because it played stage to a man whose life had been produced by Hollywood. Though he had been indoctrinated to stay on set, he become suspicious of what lay beyond its borders. Breaching a fear of the water that had been fostered since his birth, he took off in that ocean to see what he was missing. When I set out on this trip, I might have fancied a parallel with Truman. Now I know I kidded myself. Not only because I don't think it's possible to ever reach that line but also because, even if there were, if put in his position, I doubt I'd have his courage.

I look back on the line between sea and sky. It's unfair, the way the horizon's so clear and unreachable. It's unfair needing something like that.

MOBILE, ALABAMA AND WESTWARD
■■■■■■■■■■■■■■■■■■■■■■■■■■■■■■

I drive on. Out of Florida and its trappings. On west. In Mobile, my search for a cheap room
takes me to a sketchy, pier-raised motel off an abandoned
bay. There, I sift through my bags, pulling out the cutoffs I
got in a Minnesotan Goodwill, Florida's flowered Western
shirt, and a pair of brown knee-high boots from a con-
signment store in Philly. With my hair pulled into two
high curly pigtails, in Oakland this might pass as a naughty
Southern country girl getup, but I'm not sure what to call it
here in Alabama, a place pretty damn country and about as
Southern as you can get.

I've always loved Halloween. It's a day when artifice is
sublime. I also figure it might make my evening rites a little
easier than normal. Except I'm the cliché: all dressed up
with absolutely no idea where to go. I have a standing invite
from my motel's only other guests—a pair of large, hirsute
men, who, hugging red boxes of Bud and motioning to the
grill in their pickup, offered me beer, barbeque, and a good

time—but I think I'll pass. There's nothing around the motel but black water and the passing lights of the nearby freeway. The two-bit door lock looks as if it would succumb to the mere suggestion of force. I tiptoe past their room. I can hear their big, hairy laughs through the wall. I tiptoe because I don't think they need to see me dressed like this, but also because I haven't learned how to walk in my boots with the badassness they deserve.

Back in my car, I drive through Mobile, trying to find the heart of the city's nightlife. Prosperity has abandoned most of Mobile. The downtown is all low lights and dim corners. Even Dauphin Street, the main drag, has strips of darkness, the action hiccuping blocks so as not to stretch too thin. Groups walk down the street. Girls in cat ears rope their arms around each other. A couple in bedsheets stop at a corner, adjusting each other's togas. Devils and angels and nuns strut, laugh, knock hips.

At a bar promising world-famous gumbo and a costume contest, I park. The gumbo is waterier than I expected; the floating okra looks sad. I'm approached by a man who can't quite control his torso, the bar counter an axis on which his body depends. I lean away from his boozy questions, and when an older couple in rubber yellow rain suits come up to the bar, I talk them into a conversation. Before leaving for another party, they tell me to have a great night in Mobile. They make it sound like an order that's impossible to fail.

Another veering man, this one in an orange shirt with a jack-o'-lantern print, finds me. I tell him he has a half-assed costume.

"You're sassy!" he says, putting his arm around my shoulder.

"And you have an inadequate sense of personal space."

He thinks this, too, is hilarious. I excuse myself to the bathroom, checking the clock along the way. I've always abided by the rule that one must spend at least as much time out as she did getting ready: I'm a good twenty minutes short. I go back to the bar and down a scotch, hoping the spirit will improve my own.

But I'm not ready to give up. Not just yet. I walk down the street, having finally figured out how to do it in these boots. It takes a runway stride, a strut that from the outside, I imagine, just might be convincing. I pass the bald blocks, the lit bars, and people smoking outside them. Across the street, two girls in school uniforms enter a bar. Females,

I decide, are a good sign and I follow them in. The bar is populated by disco babes in polyester, eighties boys in Adidas, bunnies and bloody men, a Jolly Green Giant. Music beats under the loud banter. The bartenders pour, turn, shout amounts, and nod their recognition to those waiting with money and multiple orders. I repeat my ritual.

Sit at the bar.

Order.

Wait.

People arrive and exclaim and hug. They play with costume props, ask after friends, order more drinks. I make small talk with a few people at the bar waiting for their turns.

Eavesdrop on others.

People-watch.

Peel at the label of my beer.

Several times I get up and walk around as if I'm looking for someone. Ask the time as an attempt at conversation, or maybe so it seems my friends are just late. I go to the ladies room, hoping for the camaraderie of stall lines and lipstick. In the line outside are the two schoolgirls. They flirt with a sailor, their Southern accents rising and falling around his low drawl. I go back to the bar, stare at my bottle.

If only I knew where to look. What to do with my hands. My beer buzz only amplifies my pity trip. Why did I assume tonight would necessarily be any different? The only differences are that there are more people out with friends to make me feel worse about not having any, and that, for all the lonely drunken men, I'm now dressed to encourage them.

As if on cue, a round, red-faced man stumbles up against me. "Hey, dollface, what are you supposssed to be, besidesss gorrrgeousss?"

His Ss spray spit on my cheek. Wiping it off, I wonder if the motel's Budweiser boys are hitting their peak. I wonder what's on cable. It's been more than two hours. One more drink would do me in.

"My, if your hair ain't just the *cutest!*" a female voice says. I realize she's talking to me.

It is one of the schoolgirls. "Oh, thanks. I like yours too." Her two sandy blond pigtails are tied with red bows.

"Will you just look at that curl! Is that natural?" she asks. I nod. "My goodness, honey, you sho' are a *lucky* thing. And who you here with?"

"Um . . . myself."

"What's that?" her brunet friend asks, joining us at

the bar. They both wear white shirts tied up at the stomach, high, green pleated skirts, and white knee-highs. The brunet has an Italian complexion. The blond's hair has more wave and her body, more curve.

"Oh, I'm just passing through town and thought I'd come out."

"This your first night in Mobile? And you're here all by yo'self?" the brunet asks. I nod.

"Oh no, honey, no you ain't." The blond one throws her arm around my shoulders. "You're here with *us.*"

The bartender hands them their drinks. "Hey, Peter, look at us: In our pigtails, don't we look like sisters?" They pull away from the bar and take me with them. "What's yo' name? I'm Lucy," the fairer one says, "and this is Deb. . . . So what brings you to Mobile? Going around the country, all by yo'self? My, my, you're a brave thing, ain'tcha. . . ? And what are you supposed to be? *Honey*, if those ain't some *sweet* boots! Well, Mobile don't offer much, but we'll show you some fun, won't we?"

Lucy and Deb cradle their vowels like babies, lulling one sound into the next. Lucy, the blond, is the more outgoing of the two, but they are both generous with their affection. Within minutes, they are tugging me into pho-

tographs, their arms tight around my waist. They introduce me with half hugs to everyone they know and some
they don't.

In another hour, Lucy, Deb, and I are inseparable.
We've known each other for years, lives, beyond. And
though the alcohol may play a part—Deb is increasingly
distracted—our high also feels organic, as if our cocktails
were merely coincidence.

"I need your help, *Alicia*." I love the way Lucy says my
name. Her voice slaloms around its six letters, stretching it
into a sound that seems to say more. "You need to help me
with Deb here. See that guy over there?"

A paunchy man in a priest's collar sits in the corner.
I'd noticed him earlier. His receding, greased black hair
looks like seaweed left at low tide. He wears a gray expression and his body is a sulking mass.

"That's Deb's man. I know, he's like fifteen years older
than 'er."

"He's a *good* man," Deb pleads.

"True, she usually goes out with *real* assholes," Lucy
says, to which Deb nods. "And he's got a job and treats her
well enough. But *honey,* has he got issues."

I glance his way and he meets my eyes with a glare.

Lucy continues: "He don't like it when Deb here has any fun at all. Just look at 'im. He gets all possessive and shit. He thinks that just 'cause she's young and so pretty, he can't trust her." Deb looks away, toward the corner. Lucy puts her arms around the two of us, pulling us tighter. "But we know a *girl* has just got to be with the *girls* sometimes. So we need to make her forget about that nonsense. Shit, it's Halloween. And us girls, we need to do it up *right*."

"Okay then," Deb suddenly focuses back and declares, "let's go dancin'."

We walk down the street, one foot in front of the other as if we're on the Yellow Brick Road. "Schlemiel, Schlemazel," like Laverne and Shirley. We switch to smaller steps—I'm not the only one wearing heels too high—and use each other's shoulders for support. With someone else leaning on me, I feel featherlight.

We go to the club. Boys buy us a round. We laugh and we tease recklessly. Flirt with abandon. We make requests. Dance hard. Sing along. Occasionally, guys join in, pull one away, but by the end of the song we're always back together, sharing the drink he bought us, eyeing others we know won't last. We dance hard. Laugh hard. We drip sweat.

The night eventually unravels. We lose Deb before

finding her at another bar, half collapsed on her boyfriend's lap, his meaty hand groping up her skirt. Lucy and I continue, trying to have as much fun, but by that time, the alcohol and girl power are wearing off. Hooking-up hour has begun. We walk sock footed to our cars.

"I wish you were staying here, Alicia. You know how to have a good time."

"I wish you were coming on the road with me. We'd have a blast."

We mean it as much as we've meant anything. We mean it even as we don't. We hug goodbyes and go on our ways alone.

I wake in the morning to a dull hangover and a dozen Budweiser cans littering my motel's deck. I navigate my way past them, get back in my car, and continue west. I take several days getting to New Orleans, where I go straight to the airport to pick up my mom, who's flying in for a couple of days to see Louisiana with me.

It's a thrill checking into a hotel downtown, having conversations with someone from whose cloth I'm cut. Touring the cemeteries, we eavesdrop on the formal tours and report back to each other what we learned. At restaurants, we ask what the other's going to get and taste each other's food. We leave the city after a day and drive west and around, by the swampland, under the moss-draped trees. I like getting to say Isn't This Beautiful? out loud. Hearing her as surprised as I am to see dead armadillos on the side of the road. Going to motels with breakfast buffets and critiquing them together. I like how she calls attention to the road habits I've unconsciously acquired: my improved sense of direction, my method of opening my rear window's broken zipper, my comfort with strangers. The drawbacks—the way she keeps pronouncing "bayou" and "N'awlins," overaccented and dragged four syllables too long—are there, too. I suffer through the mere fact she's a person I have to think of when considering music, my car's open top, my acquired love of getting a little lost.

We stay at nice places, a cottage in the Bayou with a porch and rocking chairs, a cabin on a plantation off the Mississippi. Even the Best Western is a thrill. For four days we tour Louisiana, playing tourist and nothing more. It comes more easily than I expected. Perhaps too easily. I'm surprised that for all the things we see—the New Orleans street musicians, the cypress trees, even the gators and plantations' slavery remnants—none of them seem so sharp as that I've seen alone. My mother's companionship acts as a filter, softening the state we pass through. I can't decide whether Louisiana feels more pleasant or proscribed because of it.

After finishing our loop back to New Orleans, I drop my mom at the airport, assuring her I'll see her in barely three weeks' time. I return alone to a city hostel and claim a bed. I'm miserable, then thrilled. Back to despondent. For the first hour, my solitude is as exciting and horrible as it was when I first left home.

Maybe it's having experienced the mixed blessings of traveling with someone, maybe it's the length of time I've been on the road or because I'm headed back west, toward home, but the road I rejoin out of New Orleans is different from before. More open. Unapologetic. I take elevated roads over the marshes, lower onto solid ground, north into Arkansas. The lake country is easy and the driving feels so good, I continue late into the dusk. At one stretch, I pass a controlled burn of the flat, harvested fields. The earth is thick with gray smoke and low flame. It looks like a near mirror of the cloudy, red-setting sky. It looks apocalyptic. The night is hot and smoke blows through my open car; I can't get enough of its smell. Black swarms of insects flee the smoke and I turn off my music so I can listen to them. They scream as if it is the end of the world, hitting my exposed arm and thickening into a glaze on my windshield. The flames smolder around me and the smoke is sweet, and though there must be others watching over the burns, it's easy to imagine the insects are right and I'm the only one left.

I can barely see through my window in the morning—the carnage is so dense—and the attendant at the gas station eyes me as I scrub my car down, pulling away without a purchase. Through the Arkansas pines, into the town of Hot Springs, where a guy is touching up Bill's portrait on the BIRTHPLACE OF BILL CLINTON sign, back into white-barked woods. The air smells like barbeque, then scrubbed clean, of onion rings when I pass a Dairy Queen, then clean again. On west, the trees thin and the South begins giving way as Oklahoma's native names take over. I drive over the Winding Stair Mountains, full of vistas where the land takes stock in big raspy breaths, and continue back down into the flatness. Under funnels of circling vultures and through towns almost indistinguishable from the ratty brown land that surrounds them; the poverty has presence and the beauty is not an easy one.

My original itinerary didn't go this way. It wound south along the Gulf to the southeastern Texan town of Corpus Christi, a town that played host to my first beloved bad-girl road movie, *The Legend of Billie Jean*. The movie told the story of a young woman on the run who cuts her blond hair boy-short, plays a lot of Pat Benatar, and becomes a national icon—a story that gave me some of my first lessons on the importance of girl power, good soundtracks, and even better haircuts. But I've heard Corpus Christi is a pit, and instead of trekking through all those tedious Texan miles, I decide to take the advice of another pair of female outlaws by avoiding the state altogether. Along with Billie Jean, Bush, and the Dallas Cowboys, Thelma and Louise have made Texas a state I feel free to begrudge. I study the map, trying to figure a way around its obesity. The state looks to be everything that's wrong with America: Proud. Gluttonous. Spoiled. My dislike is strong and simple.

I'm not sure why, then, I pass the road that would take me north into Oklahoma's panhandle and head straight into Texas. Maybe it's curiosity or the fact that I like the route I'm on, with its fabulous straightaways and the way its generic towns are less common than the raw, ornery ones. Maybe I just feel due for another WELCOME TO . . . sign. Three months and thirty-one states in, they still thrill me.

As if on purpose, Texas denies me that satisfaction, my route devolving into farm roads too small to warrant a sign. I pass cattle farms whose density and reek make even an unrepentant carnivore like me wince. Cotton crops lay half harvested, some fields puffs of white, others revealing their naked, thorny stems. Tumbleweeds—those I'd previously seen only in *Peanuts* cartoons—lie trapped in fences.

Across the country, I've seen the many forms poverty can take: the Midwestern deprecating sadness, the scrappiness in urban ghettos, how it hung lethargic in the Southern air. But with all this space, the horizon promising all that the West would seem to offer, the knocks here feel less forgiving.

And perhaps it shouldn't, but it floors me. The land is hard and the wind is hot and the road is tough and ugly and, yes, sexy as all hell.

I take a few photos as I drive. A nondescript store in Turkey, Texas. A stiff windmill that should have long ago been recycled for its scrap metal. I angle my camera on the dashboard and set the timer, taking a picture of myself as I drive. I feel a little like the road: a little tough, a little ugly, and, yes, damn sexy, too. My hair is horrible, my knotted curls fried, sun-bleached straight, and snapped short in the front. The past few hundred miles of dust and gnat and manure have stormed through my car and accumulated on my skin. Though my body has the same give it's always had, my tan makes me feel firmer. I squint as the sun lowers and the shutter snaps, revealing wrinkles that, at the moment, I think becoming.

In the last scene of *Terminator,* Linda Hamilton is photographed at a desolate Mexican gas station, sitting in her open Jeep, talking into a tape recorder for her future son. I pick up my own recorder. "Should I tell you about your father?" I say. "That's a tough one."

Near the end of the day in a bland town, I pass several of Texas's drive-through liquor stores. I pull into one, plan my abandon. A sign posts the new state law that it's illegal to drink while driving. I'd thought it was still legal here, but buying a six-pack, I thought it was just as well; its lawfulness would thwart my purpose.

Back on the road, I crack one open. Never mind I'm only going about ten miles to Hereford to get a motel for the night. Or that I refrain from drinking when I'm passing other cars. Or that my inspiration is a tired road cliché, and that I'm an outrageous dork for letting this excite me. Sunglasses on, Benatar turned high, I finish the can, crunch it in my hand, and throw it on the passenger seat floor. It still makes me high.

CHAPTER TWELVE

Thelma and Louise

THELMA
Okay, then listen, let's not get caught.

LOUISE
What are you talking about?

THELMA
Let's keep going.

[THELMA AND LOUISE]

So, I'm no Billie Jean. I'm no Thelma and I'm no Louise. That empty beer can? I didn't even last into the city limits before my good sense won out, hiding the evidence at the bottom of my trash bag. But then, those girls had the advantage of being on the wrong side of the law. My trespasses—one beer, a liberal reading of posted speed limits, and a mild case of indecent exposure—are hardly the foundation of the fuck-it-all freedom they so gloriously achieved.

Still, the West is good to me. Surrounded by so much open land, I feel less restrained. My night in Texas is not a highlight: After sitting at a beef joint, poking at my plate made from a suspicious salad bar while the regulars openly gape at me, I retreat to a motel I've been warned against. I spend the night sitting at the foot of the bed, drinking Bud and clicking channels on the remoteless TV. In the morning, my car is a getaway. I head out of Texas on a numbered road, past more gray land, until a sign designates a shift in county and state: NEW MEXICO. Almost immediately, the ground drops. Erosion rips into the red dirt. The industrial smells of Texas turn earthy. The last several states' plateau suddenly feels like an illusion, and the surprise makes me whoop out loud.

It's unfair how everything is striking when it's fleeting. Yet all my attempts to thwart this, trying to prolong a moment by stopping to savor a town or view, tend only to prove it true, the high ache of passing a place collapsing the moment I try to capture it. Strangers make me self-conscious. Expectations interfere. Rather than slowing time, I only make it awkward. So now, as I drive, I try to ride that heartbreak, accepting that the very thing that makes this moment spectacular is that which will make it end. As I wind west and north through New Mexico, the land is open and the road is mine.

My route takes me north into the empty high desert, through the craggy Sangre de Cristo Mountains, and into Taos, where chili lights border shop windows and Southwestern motifs decorate art galleries. White people in fringy Indian jackets walk down the street.

Taos lacks all of the grit I've swooned over recently. It does, on the other hand, have coffee shops. And its hippies don't intimidate me. Driving into Taos, I feel comfortable enough to pass judgment on it, and I instantly know that for all the sex appeal of the more severe landscapes, this place is embarrassingly, unflatteringly more like me.

In the morning, I chat with a café owner, Mikey. He looks like a younger, slighter Kevin Spacey and tells me excitedly of his many business prospects and invention ideas, his herbal concoctions and bagels with cheese baked inside. Mikey's animated. Rather, he's hyper and a tad manic, but he's cute enough, and I like not having to carry the conversation.

"So what've you got planned for your day?" he asks.

"Someone at the hostel told me there was a hot spring off the river. I couldn't find it last night—it got too dark—but I thought I'd try again."

"I was just on my way there myself," Mikey beams. "I go there most every day. If you'd like a ride down, I'd be happy for the company."

Mikey shows me to his car, a beat-up Corolla with a backseat of trash. The hot spring is across the Rio Grande and down a dirt road. The walls of the canyon tower over the relatively narrow river, and, following Mikey down a path, I can smell the sulfur coming from the small spring-fed pool by its banks, a slight steam rising off it. I take care not to look at Mikey as he strips naked. I'd normally do the same, but considering I'm with someone I've known barely twenty minutes, I'm glad to have my suit.

The water is nicely warm, if not as hot as it could be. I lean back on the rocks and close my eyes as Mikey tells me of the water's ancient healing properties. I half wish I was alone or that he'd shut up, but I also like how his voice distracts me from my thoughts. The spring's source is a dull glow of heat on my right, and I swirl the warmer water around me.

After a half hour or so of soaking, Mikey suggests I try something. He has me lie back on his hands while the rest of my body floats. He leans my head back in the water so his voice is only a murmur and puts pressure on my neck, my shoulders, my high spine. Moves down my back. Some time later, midway down my back, he lowers my top. I consider it, tug it back up. It was just getting in the way, he explains. Arms, wrists, hands, lower back. Steady pressure then a slow massage. A while later, when he returns to the same part of my back, I concede and lower it for him.

I keep my eyes closed throughout, listening to the water, the occasional mumble of his voice. He moves on to my lower body, my feet, my ankles, my calves. Occasionally, I wonder how this looks, but most of my thoughts feel far away. I feel pressure between my legs. My eyes closed, I lose myself in what is hand, finger, until later, my suit bottoms pulled aside, there is the unmistakable feel of mouth. I lie back and enjoy it.

When Mikey finally pulls me up into a hug, I pretend I don't feel him hard against me. Were he a little less chatty. Were he Brad Pitt. But instead he acts as if he were on uppers and he smells like old herbs and BO. He and his erection watch me dry off. I feign blindness to both.

We've just finished gathering our stuff and are on our way up the path when I see two large Latino men carrying towels, coming toward the pool. *Just in time,* I think. Then I see the smiles they greet me with. They look like they enjoyed the show.

■ ■■■■■■■■■

Back when I left home those three and a half months ago, I thought I'd talked myself out of the road myth. Thought that romanticism was something that could be rationalized away. But, of course, I never really forsook the freedom it promised; I just renamed it. I told myself I was searching for realism and thought this made my search different. But what was I really looking for? Freedom from my expectations, from my romanticism. A freedom that would give me control over what I wanted. Now I'm not so sure abandon works that way.

Still, if my cynicism has gotten in the way of my honesty, it has had one nice kickback. The places where the road's glory's proven true, I've felt positively heady. After picking my way north and west into Colorado on green dotted routes that someone's officially sanctioned as scenic, I veer up on Route 141, which makes no such promises. I find it's more spectacular for the lack of endorsement. The road winds down through rusty terraced rocks, taking its time. The colors of sky and earth, turquoise and brick are wildly well suited. Domestication comes only in traces—a few cows on the roadside, staring at me as if I'm the strange one, turnoffs with no apparent destination—and the land's texture and scale are alien. I follow the road into a canyon and along a river, staring at the sandstone that looms above me and plummets into a gash below, teasing my ability to take in only one at a time.

Many would cross this red earth and correctly associate it with all the old westerns filmed here. Cowboys and Indians, swaggering John Wayne, grizzled Clint Eastwood: a land of hard men and manly land. For me, though, two women ride like ghosts through this landscape. I've taken this two-hour detour through Colorado because Route 141 was listed in the *Thelma and Louise* filming locations. Yes, I'll concede now, I've chosen a strange way to fight my expectations. And driving this road I'm occasionally distracted, wondering if this is where they locked the cop in his trunk or pulled over at dawn to appreciate the view.

But while I still have questions—*How would it be to see this with a partner in crime? How did they avoid passing any of the area's tourist stores and chain gas stations?*—right now, I don't mind so much, either. I'm just glad they got me on this road. And maybe my time on the road's getting to me, but these ghosts, I feel no urge to flee. To be honest, I almost like their company.

I continue up through Grand Junction, where the land yellows and flattens, joining up with a six-lane interstate where my speedometer hits one hundred thousand miles. I'm proud I can claim almost thirteen thousand as my own. The freeway's pace is sadistic, and my urge to get off it is no longer just a matter of preference. The end of this trip is so near. Every mile on a freeway feels like a waste. I get off on a farm road that parallels the freeway before turning south to Moab, onto another road used in the movie. A dusty plateau. A deserted town. Back into a half-eroded scope of red and rock and road. Civilization stretches no wider than the road. The sky is electric. I'd think I'd begin to tire of it. But once again, my reaction is visceral, almost violent. Not like the violence of the screen—innumerable and numb—but the kind you experience firsthand, the kind whose force wrecks you with just how brief it all is.

I wrap myself in my jacket and scarf so I can keep the top back and the windows unrolled, the better to let it surround me. I know better now than to stop, though it still hurts. My skin feels as sensitive as my fingertips, and my ribs ache from the pressure in my chest. This is better than the hot spring. I play a throbbing song and scream along in my car. My heart swirls as furiously in my head as my hair does in the wind. Cars pass me as I beat my steering wheel, raise my arms, and dance. I don't begin to do it justice.

In the movie, Thelma and Louise ended their journey surrounded by cops, driving off the cliffs of the Grand Canyon, soaring to their deaths. The next morning, in my Moab hostel, I pull out my map. Whether because of the Canyon's red tape or the Park Service's concern for the ecological impact of a '66 Thunderbird, *Thelma and Louise*'s director, Ridley Scott, actually filmed the finale at a nearby point in Utah's Canyonlands called Dead Horse Point. All the dots on my map snake together save one. The Point lies alone like an exclamation.

Dead Horse Point's shape loosely resembles a three-legged turtle. Two thousand precipitous feet over the Colorado River's canyon, the mesa has a round body with several short outcroppings and a head of sandstone connected by a thirty-yard "neck." Legend has it that cowboys used to corral wild mustangs on this peninsula, blocking off the neck so they could pick out the horses they preferred. Once, the mustangs were left there with no water; the land's name tells the rest.

Turning off the freeway for the park, I'm surprised I'm excited. It's a beautiful day and the road is nicely vacant. Though these many weeks on the road have dulled my anticipation of movie locations, approaching this one, I feel as if it's my first. It's a battle to drive slow and savor it.

I get no farther than the Dead Horse State Park booth, however, than my recurrent issues kick in. The parking lot is noisy with two touring vans. After all these months, I still tighten up at the paved vistas, at the people angling their photos around them. I try to shake it off by leaving my car at the rangers station and walking the empty two-mile trail around the Dead Horse Point head.

I follow the trail's cairns over rocks and the red dirt, trying to mind the warnings not to step on the unbroken soil, battling vertigo the times I come close to the edge. The views are tremendous; it looks like I imagine the Grand Canyon's looking, the gorge so vast and distant it's almost two dimensional. My trail continues around the head, beside the asphalt road and into busy vistas. Using crosswalks, I feel ridiculous pretending I'm in the wild, but I try to appreciate it just the same. Take some shots. Try to take it in. Below, I can see an appealing dirt road and the dirty blue path of the Colorado. A salt plant's drying beds flank a part of the river, rectangles of phosphorescent green. Really, though, the only thing my hike makes me feel is a wish to finish it.

I'm not too disappointed, though, because this isn't actually where those women drove off. That scene was shot on Shafer Trial, a road that winds around this peak on a flat ridge a thousand or so feet lower. My map shows a shortcut to the trail, and back at the rangers station, I consult with them on how to get to it. They tell me the road's pretty rough, but as long as I have four-wheel drive, I should be fine.

Following their instructions, I turn right on a dirt road a quarter mile after the park exit. They weren't kidding. This road is bad. Really bad. It leads off into the desert, not much more than a groove of tire tracks between a clearing of shrubs. My tires kick up a fine dust that coats the insides of my open car. My dashboard, mirror, vents, sunglasses, skin—everything is covered in red.

I rumble slowly through the sand, half suspecting I'm on the wrong road but going ahead anyway. Twice, my tires spin in the dust before catching stronger ground and moving out, and though I think I should be descending into the canyon anytime, the plateau's edge is just out of sight. It makes me feel as if I'm driving on borrowed land. As if I'm about to discover the edge in a most unfortunate way. After ten more minutes, the road devolves into nothing. Sand and shrubs spread as far as I can see. The few tire tracks veer in different deserted directions. This can't be right. Screw it: I turn around.

I make it about a quarter of the way back to the main road when my tires hit a soft patch and can't spin themselves out.

I stop, gas it again.

The rubber and sand sound like chafing corduroy.

Fortunately, I've got four-wheel drive. Unfortunately, when I told the rangers I had all-wheel drive, I failed to mention that I've never used it before. I try shifting it on but it won't click in, or it seems to but makes no difference, my wheels spinning deeper and deeper in the dust.

I try it three, five, ten times before getting out and digging at the sand. Try again. Save the kicking dust, the desert remains stationary. I look for rocks to wedge under my tires. Some look solid enough, but when I touch them, they disintegrate into dust.

I open the glove compartment and pull out my owner's manual. It says my manual free-wheeling hubs must be locked for the all-wheel drive to engage. It might as well have been written in Japanese, for as much sense as that made.

In *Thelma and Louise,* Louise once said, "Well, we're not in nowhere, but we can see it from here." I see it surrounding me.

I stare at the expanse of sand. At the half inch of water left in my bottle. I'm probably no more than three or four miles from the park road, another two or three to the rangers' station, maybe not even that. I actually feel pretty calm, considering my options.

My hands, however, betray me. They tremble as I scoop away more sand. My bladder, too; it suddenly can't stand the pressure. In a stroke of what I think is brilliance, I squat close to the channels I've dug out behind my back tires, hoping the liquid will give the sand more traction. So, I'm no Thelma or Louise. I'm no MacGyver either. My tires spin some more.

I should just start walking, but I'm not yet convinced this is happening to me. I give my four-wheel drive a few more gos. Then a couple of dozen more. I don't know if I do something differently, or maybe my urine trick has a delayed effect, but with a noise as beautiful as any I've heard, the gear clicks in and my car lurches out.

Fifteen minutes later, I'm back on pavement. I drive for no more than a few hundred yards when, on my right, I see a wide dirt road. A real road.

It, too, is rough. Rutted into hard, narrow channels, it feels as if it's been lined with Spanish roof tiles. Driving over it, I ache for a sports bra, but compared to my last detour, it's a fun ride. Eventually descending from the mesa, the road deteriorates into a one-car pass through cut-out sandstone. The road's gutted holes and lumped mounds tilt my car back and forth—I imagine riding an elephant would feel similar—and for the fifth time in as many days, I appreciate the fact that I'm alone. Most of my friends would have enough sense to talk me out of these roads. Rock looms over me, next to me, shakes my body, sticks to my skin. It makes my heart beat faster.

When at last I come to Shafer Trail, my joints relax with the improved conditions. I follow the trail around the Colorado's curves, passing the salt plant, the dirt clearings that appear every few hundred yards, looking out onto the gorge. Pulling over at a few, I study their size and flatness, considering how the view would look from a '66 Thunderbird and how many cop cars they could fit. Many of them feel familiar, but none are any more recognizable than that. I backtrack to one of the bigger and more tire-tracked ones, pulling as close to the edge as fear of heights and getting stuck will allow. I put my car in neutral and let my engine idle.

When I first saw *Thelma and Louise* with friends, I remember a few of them being crushed by the closing shot of the blue Thunderbird sailing into the canyon, craving instead the equivalent of a romantic comedy's last kiss: Fast-forward two years, the two women living the life we all knew they couldn't reach, sipping margaritas by the Mexican seaside. At the time, I argued it couldn't have ended any other way. That the way they faded away midflight, their dual suicide actually felt remarkably happily ever after. But I understood. The movie got them—as it did me—and it felt unfair that the women's decision to keep going was their only way out.

The canyon's overlapping walls recede in front of me. The remnants of a campfire lie nearby. For as badass and alive as I felt getting to this road, I feel just as dorky and bored now that I'm here. Plus, though none of the dozen others I checked out seemed any better, I harbor the same suspicion that this isn't the right pullout as I did that that first dirt road was not the right road. And it bothers me. Even if I know finding the exact spot won't answer the question of why I need to, it bothers me to have come all this way and not be sure.

I sit in my car, staring out at the canyon. I feel more stuck than I did thirty minutes ago, surrounded by nowhere, pawing at the sand. I can't shake the feeling that if I don't find what I'm looking for, I'm still meant to find something equally satisfying. My car idles. The canyon, stretching ahead of me, is so still it seems dead. I can know that expectations are unavoidable; that there is no ending save the one Thelma and Louise drove into; that aiming for something is better than not having reached at all. But they feel like trite consolations for my failure to find that spot, like knee-jerk Hollywood morals born less from any real growth than from my nostalgia for moments five minutes past, when I was rumbling down that road and the red dirt rocked my car, spun in my hair. When the ending was something to root for but the real joy was losing myself in the rapture of pursuit, and happily ever after was just a fade-out away.

Homebound

My itinerary hinging only on getting home by Thanksgiving in one week's time, budget and whim steer my course west. After one more day in Moab's Canyonlands, I move south through the Valley of Gods, taking another dirt road into Arizona and the recognizable towers of Monument Valley. The land is as scenic and dramatic as a car commercial, but whether I'm numbed by the Canyonlands or changed by my new lack of purpose, nothing seems significant. As I drive on, the land shifts colors and textures; I cease tracking the changes. A restless sleep in a Flagstaff hostel of drunken *Real World* wannabes cements the fact: I'm ready for home.

Through Arizona, I'm forced onto freeway and take detours through scenic routes that don't deserve their title. The land is flat and Wal-Marted. The road is unremarkable. I'm almost tempted to just shoot straight through to Oakland when, in the afternoon, I reach a small road through Nevada's southern tip. It's as ugly as I expect it to be but back in that way I love. It in turn leads me to the Joshua Tree freeway. Endless, in every direction, the Joshuas raise their hairy, knobbed arms, as if frozen in a Dr. Seuss dance. The desert is a massive party and I turn up my music to join it. The road is even and empty. This is the road I can't get enough of. This is the feeling I'm going to miss.

As I come into California, into the Mojave, the cacti disappear as quickly as they arrived. The road, though, is still straight and spectacularly minimal. Tonight, word goes, is the Leonid Meteor Shower, the biggest meteor storm in thirty-five years, and I can't imagine a better place to watch it. As I come down into a wide, barren plain, a collection of buildings lies on my left, three or four in total, and I slow down.

Nipton, California, "conveniently located in the middle of nowhere," was once the hideaway of the silent film legend, Clara Bow. Now it is a B&B with a cantina and tent cabins surrounded by 1.7 million acres of Mojave. Several couples and a family have booked all the cabins for the meteor shower, but the genial man at the gift store says for a small fee, I can camp anywhere I'd like. He even has a sleeping pad I can use. I drive over a ridge, a quarter mile out into the desert, and set up my tent.

HOMEBOUND

I've just gotten into bed and am listening to the silence of the desert when I hear a distant rumble. The noise grows closer and deeper until it roars from the earth, making both air and ground shake. It seems the middle of nowhere has a train track running through it. The train's horn rises to a scream, a noise as haunting and industrial as man's power can be, and yet it also feels as organic as the soil itself, as if it belongs here.

At 2:00 AM, I fight the cold, get out with my sleeping bag and onto the hood of my car. I look up; the sky seems impossibly big. I see a few quick flashes in my peripheral vision. I feel as if I'm just missing them. Within half an hour, though, the whole of the sky is a canvas. I can hear those in the cabins across the desert *oooh*ing as I do. Some streaks are needle thin, silver fine-point scratched in the sky. Others look painted by brushes, bright swaths that burn my eyes.

The next few days will be just as fleeting. My trip's lack of car problems will make up for lost time. Tomorrow I'll wake up to a flat tire. Two days later, coming down a mountain, when my warning lights flash and my car starts to smoke, I'll realize I haven't checked my oil since Georgia. Two days after that, I'll fishtail my way through a snowstorm in the Sierras, doing a full 180 to face the car behind me before I drive back to get chains. I will sleep in a trailer park in Tecopa, an empty, historic hotel in Independence, a hostel in Mammoth Springs, where I'll spend the night sharing a wall with a couple of amorous guests, wishing the woman weren't so vocal and the man didn't have such staying power. I will love Death Valley, its severity, its white dunes and pink rocks, the fact that I can park wherever, climb a few crags, and lie alone in the sun. The salt spires of Mono Lake will be arresting, the Sierras, sharp and white. In four days, on Thanksgiving morning, I'll be pulling back into Oakland, reuniting with hugs and questions about this trip I took, my favorite places and people. I'll find myself explaining it with stock phrases, the few scenic photos I took, with anecdotes that don't seem to amount to much.

In weeks, I'll be back waitressing. And in months that quickly accrue into years, I'll be in back in a place, at least on paper, remarkably similar to that which I left. I'll still not have found love. I won't meet new people as I did on the road because I won't need to, and I'll try to remember what it was like when I did, fighting not to make it grander in the retelling. And almost three years from the time I originally left for my road trip, with the Moab dust still clinging to parts of my car, I'll be leaving again. Wondering if I've learned a damn thing, I'll be packing my bags, moving to New York. I'll cringe at my transparency: Really, if I am going to continue mocking these romantic clichés, I ought to quit chasing them. But if I believe in anything stronger than the foolishness of my expectations, it's in the hope that this time I will thwart them. Or failing that, if I'm lucky, maybe I'll glimpse something real and wondrous in the moments in between.

HOMEBOUND

But right now, the night is spitting stars. And while the streaks burn fast and bright, much lower, another light hurtles through the Mojave. The train's wail fills the dark and rumbles the earth. It's only a trace of what moves me.

Acknowledgments

To all those who offered shelter and companionship along the way—Katsy, Maggie, Jessica, Motsy, Brian, the whole Montgomery clan, Amy, Katie, Mark, and Kristie—you made futons and pullouts feel like magic. Ditto for all those I met on the road: Shelly, Bill, Matt, Toussant, Detroit, Patrick, Brian, Lucy, Deb, and all the other pseudonyms that didn't make it to the page.

I want to thank The San Francisco Foundation and Intersection for the Arts for their support and encouragement. Salon and AlterNet, Don George, and Hazen for the same.

To Brooke Warner and the Seal crew: Thanks for giving this a good home. Helen and Bobbie and Claire and Trevor and Gary and the others who suffered through the early drafts: Your input was invaluable. Special shout-out to Stephanie Kip Rosten. Go Socks.

Along the way, rent was paid, and for making that such a bearable and, at times, inexcusably enjoyable process, I owe a lot to the crews of Garibaldi's and Markt.

I'm spoiled by the friendships of Daisy and Meghan. Brooke and Maggie. Ciara. Aida. Anais. You're the reason I think *Stand by Me* had it wrong.

I want to thank the Adams family at large, particularly Martha, for the gift of Guerneville. Mom, your support is extraordinary, especially when it goes against your better judgment. Dad, where would I be without your continued assurance of bail money?

And finally, to Garrette Scott, who taught me so much: You're sorely missed.

About the Author

© TIM WILSON

Alicia Rebensdorf has been published in Salon.com, the *Los Angeles Times,* and *Wanderlust,* Salon's travel anthology. She has worked for NPR's "On the Media" and headed the MediaCulture department at AlterNet. In 2003, she was honored with the Mary J. Tanenbaum award, an annual nonfiction award given by The San Francisco Foundation to young writers for works in progress. She lives in Brooklyn.

Selected Titles from Seal Press

For more than thirty years, Seal Press has published groundbreaking books.
By women. For women. Visit our website at www.sealpress.com.

She's Such a Geek: Women Write About Science, Technology, and Other Nerdy Stuff edited by Annalee Newitz and Charlie Anders. $14.95, 1-58005-190-1. From comic books and gaming to science fiction and blogging, nerdy women have their say in this witty collection that takes on the "boys only" clubs and celebrates a woman's geek spirit.

Woman's Best Friend: Women Writers on the Dogs in Their Lives edited by Megan McMorris. $14.95, 1-58005-163-4. An offbeat and poignant collection about those four-legged friends girls can't do without.

Dirty Sugar Cookies: Culinary Observations, Questionable Taste by Ayun Halliday. $14.95, 1-58005-150-2. Ayun Halliday is back with comical and unpredictable essays about her disastrous track record in the kitchen and her culinary observations—though she's clearly no expert.

What Would Murphy Brown Do? How the Women of Prime Time Changed Our Lives by Allison Klein. $16.95, 1-58005-171-5. From workplace politics to single motherhood to designer heels in the city, revisit TV's favorite—and most influential—women of the 1970s through today who stood up and held their own.

Bento Box in the Heartland: My Japanese Girlhood in White-bread America by Linda Furiya. $15.95, 1-58005-191-X. A uniquely American story about girlhood, identity, assimilation—and the love of homemade food.

The Anti 9-to-5 Guide: Practical Career Advice for Women Who Think Outside the Cube by Michelle Goodman. $14.95, 1-58005-186-3. Escape the wage-slave trap of your cubicle with Goodman's hip career advice on creating your dream job and navigating the work world without compromising your aspirations.